GLBTQ*

The Survival Guide for Queer & Questioning Teens

P9-DGZ-027

*Gay • **Lesbian** • **Bisexual** • **Transgender** • **Questioning**

GLBTQ*

The Survival Guide for Queer & Questioning Teens

*Gay • Lesbian • Bisexual • Transgender • Questioning

Kelly Huegel

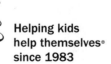

free spirit
PUBLiSHiNG®

Helping kids
help themselves®
since 1983

LIBRARY
FRANKLIN PIERCE UNIVERSITY
RINDGE, NH 03461

Library of Congress Cataloging-in-Publication Data
Huegel, Kelly, 1974–
GLBTQ* (Gay, Lesbian, Bisexual, Transgender, Questioning) : the survival guide for queer and questioning teens / Kelly Huegel.
   p. cm.
Summary: Describes the challenges faced by gay, lesbian, bisexual, and transgendered teens, offers practical advice, real-life experiences, and accessible resources and support groups.
 Includes bibliographical references and index.
 ISBN 1-57542-126-7
1. Homosexuality—United States—Juvenile literature. 2. Coming out (Sexual orientation)—United States—Juvenile literature. 3. Gay teenagers—United States—Juvenile literature. 4. Lesbian teenagers—United States—Juvenile literature. 5. Transsexuals—United States—Juvenile literature. 6. Bisexuals—United States—Juvenile literature. [1. Homosexuality.]
I. Title: Survival guide for queer and questioning teens. II. Title.
 HQ76.25.H84 2003
 306.76'6—dc21

                                                                        2002156692

At the time of this book's publication, all facts and figures cited are the most current available. All telephone numbers, addresses, and Web site URLs are accurate and active; all publications, organizations, Web sites, and other resources exist as described in this book; and all have been verified as of December 2007. The author and Free Spirit Publishing make no warranty or guarantee concerning the information and materials given out by organizations or content found at Web sites, and we are not responsible for any changes that occur after this book's publication. If you find an error or believe that a resource listed here is not as described, please contact Free Spirit Publishing. Parents, teachers, and other adults: We strongly urge you to monitor children's use of the Internet.

The people depicted on the cover and throughout this book are models, and are used for illustrative purposes only. The names of the teens and young adults quoted throughout the book have been changed to protect their privacy.

Edited by Dennis Cass and Jennifer Brannen
Cover and interior design by Marieka Heinlen
Index by Ina Gravitz

10 9 8 7 6 5
Printed in the United States of America

Free Spirit Publishing Inc.
217 Fifth Avenue North, Suite 200
Minneapolis, MN 55401-1299
(612) 338-2068
help4kids@freespirit.com
www.freespirit.com

Dedication

For my parents, for their unwavering support.
For Amy, for everything.
And for Joan Van Stone, the quintessential PFLAG mom, whose tireless
efforts have strengthened and reunited so many families.

Acknowledgments

Now begins the daunting task of attempting to thank everyone who contributed, in some way, to the creation of this book.

Thank you, first, to those who have gone before—GLBTQ and straight alike—and have fought to make this world a more accepting place. Your efforts have not always had an obvious reward, but your successes are evident in many ways, such as the fact that a book like this can exist.

Thanks are due to Free Spirit, who was willing to let me talk about things GLBTQ teens need to know but would make other publishers shy away.

Thank you to Steven Cozza, who took time from his very busy schedule and training to pen the foreword. Thanks also, Steven, for the fantastic work you're doing.

That my manuscript graduated to a finished book is due in large part to the efforts of Dennis Cass, a splendid and creative editor with good humor to spare. Many thanks for helping to render an at times arduous process enjoyable.

To the many, many people who contributed to this book, I offer my appreciation. Thanks also to those who took time out of their harrowingly busy schedules to share their ideas and insights. Special thanks to Jessica Xavier at the Whitman Walker Clinic; Scott Hirschfeld at GLSEN; Chris Kryzan at OUTProud; Jean Richter at the P.E.R.S.O.N. Project; Kirsten Kingdon at National PFLAG; Joan Van Stone, Barbara Warner, and Rhonda Buckner at Metro DC PFLAG; Margaux Delotte-Bennett and Tracee Ford at SMYAL; Cathy Renna at GLAAD; Caitlyn Ryan and Sandy Loiterstein for their feedback and suggestions.

Most importantly, thank you to my amazing friends and family:

There are no words to express the depth of my love and appreciation for my partner, Amy. In large ways and in small—from accepting a writer's wages (or lack thereof) to reading and offering comments on countless iterations of the chapters herein—her support of this project has never wavered.

To my parents, Jane and Dave, who might as well have written the definition of "unconditional love." We have come a long way together, and I'm proud not only to call you my parents but also to count you among my closest friends.

To my sister, Monica, many thanks for the cheerleading and comic relief. Be careful what you wish for . . . some day you might actually start to look like the older one.

To my many wonderful friends, thank you for your relentless sarcasm and biting commentary . . . I love every minute of it. The amount of laughter in my life should be illegal, and all of you are to blame. Thanks and love to Sue and David, who coined the phrase "Hey, gays!" and whose soon-to-arrive children I can't wait to spoil completely. To Becky, my partner in crime, for always lending an ear, two when necessary. To Kirby and Dan, two huge Gubios whose fantastical notions are never in short supply. To David, who I simply adore. To George, the male sister I never had. To JB, for teaching me many valuable lessons . . . like how to fan—love your show. To Paul, whose heart is so big I am amazed it fits in that compact (yet buff) package. To Shannon and Nikki, for their relative sanity and lots of girl talk. Thanks also to: Tanya "Grace"; Sarah; Alison; Megan and Brian; Steffie and Bruce; Jen-T; Sue; Kate and Alex (who is NOT English); Jenne and Shawn; Joan, Jim, Jimmy and Augie; Lany (or –ie, if you insist) and Bill; Kelly and Kathy; AJ; John and George; "Ma" Bell; Shane (and Annette, when we finally reach Sweden); Dennis and Cheryl; and so on. I apologize for anyone I may have neglected to mention—the slight was not intentional.

And finally, I offer my deepest gratitude to the young people who lent their voices to this book. The spirit and courage of these and other GLBTQ teens is truly inspiring. When we look at them, we see the future, and it gives us hope.

CONTENTS

FOREWORD

I founded Scouting for All in 1998 when I was 13 years old because I believed that the Boy Scouts of America's policy banning homosexuals was wrong. As an Eagle Scout, I failed to understand how the Boy Scouts of America (BSA), who are supposed to represent the very best of our society, embrace the very worst. Their policy of discrimination teaches Scouts to discriminate. I was (and still am) ashamed of that and decided to take a stand against this hurtful policy. Scouting for All is working to change BSA policies so that all youth, regardless of their sexual orientation, will be able to participate in Scouting.

Like me, you may have run into some homophobic, sexist, and bigoted institutions and individuals. It can help to remember that for every one of them, there are many more of us—people who accept you and care about you. You are not alone.

Being gay is normal. Being lesbian is normal. Being bisexual is normal. Being transgender is normal. Being heterosexual is normal. In a world where people are often surrounded by misleading ideas and "facts" about what it means to be gay, lesbian, bisexual, or transgender, it can be difficult to accept yourself for who you are—a normal person. Chances are, you have been exposed to some of this misinformation, too. However, there are resources that can help you understand what being queer means and what queer people are like, and this book is one of them.

GLBTQ: The Survival Guide for Queer and Questioning Teens addresses the concerns and questions GLBTQ youth face every day. There are other teens just like you who have faced many of the same issues you're facing now. This book helps to dispel the myths surrounding gay, lesbian, bisexual, and transgender teens and, in doing so, advocates on behalf of GLBTQ teens and helps them advocate for themselves. This is more than an educational resource that can be used by everyone. This book gives GLBTQ youth a real voice.

Kelly Huegel has written a truly inspiring book. She has demonstrated her own courage by speaking out on a subject many in our society don't want to talk about. If you feel alone, hopeless, or confused, I hope that by reading this book you will find comfort, information, and support. I hope you will feel empowered to be the wonderful person you were born to be. GLBTQ youth should expect the same human rights that are afforded to everyone else in our society. You shouldn't accept anything less.

Steven Cozza, Eagle Scout
Cofounder of Scouting for All
www.scoutingforall.org

INTRODUCTION

Dealing with the realization that you are or might be gay, lesbian, bisexual, transgender, or questioning (GLBTQ) can be a real challenge. And I know just how it feels. Starting in elementary school, I always had a feeling that I was not quite like my friends. By high school, I was convinced I was somehow different from everyone else, and not in a good way.

When I got to college, I met some people who I knew were GLBTQ. My feelings started to make sense, like I'd finally found the missing piece to a big puzzle. But the thought that I might actually be a lesbian frightened me a lot. What would my family and friends say? How could I live "that kind" of life? Feeling hopeless, terrified of telling anyone what I was going through, I decided the only answer was to end my life.

One night I took an overdose of pills. But then something happened. From somewhere deep down inside of me I heard a voice that told me I had to live. That no matter what happened, no matter how hard my life was going to be, it was a life worth living.

I asked someone to take me to the hospital. Now, nearly a decade later, my life is completely different. I have the love and support of my family. I have a long-time partner. Life can still be challenging at times, but I'm grateful to have it.

The journey from a confused, scared teen to the self-assured person I am today was a road traveled not by big leaps, but instead by many small steps. Fortunately, as I've grown more accepting of myself, I've been able to get involved with helping other GLBTQ people and their families learn to love and accept themselves and each other. Through my work with PFLAG (Parents, Families and Friends of Lesbians and Gays), I've talked to teens terrified about coming out. I've counseled upset parents whose children have just told them they're GLBTQ. It's been amazing to watch these teens and families go

1

from confusion and anger to a sense of acceptance and joy about who they are.

As a GLBTQ teen, life can sometimes feel pretty lonely. It's easy to think no one cares about what you're going through, but that's not true. All over the world, GLBTQ people, parents, friends, family members, and politicians are working toward creating a better understanding and acceptance of GLBTQ people. A lot of their efforts are focused on helping teens. PFLAG has made school safety one of its primary concerns. The Gay, Lesbian and Straight Education Network (GLSEN) is focused entirely on improving the school environment for GLBTQ kids. The Gay and Lesbian Alliance Against Defamation (GLAAD) is fighting for more positive and accurate messages about GLBTQ people in the media.

These are just a few examples. There are other national and local organizations where everyday people are making extraordinary progress in fighting for your rights. They're educating school boards, principals, teachers, and other school staff. They're holding in-school workshops and lobbying for better legislation at state capitols and in Washington, D.C. Progress is being made. It's happening slowly, but life for GLBTQ people is getting better.

You might be thinking, "That's great, but what about right now? What about *my* school?" It's easy to say that everything will be okay someday, or that this is just a part of growing up, or that in the future you might even look back at some of this and laugh. But those kinds of reassurances don't help you very much right now.

That's the reason I wrote this book. I remember what it was like— the worries, insecurities, and fears. One moment you might be upset about the grade you got on your history quiz, the next you're thinking about big questions like what you want to do with your life. And what if, on top of all that, you suddenly discover you're attracted to someone of the same sex? Or what if you dread changing for gym class because you're in the boys' locker room, but inside you've always felt more like a girl?

Discovering that you might be GLBTQ is a pretty big revelation and accepting it is a process. One thing that can help that process is information. This book can't answer all of your questions or counter all of the misinformation, misconceptions, half-truths, and even outright lies floating around in the world right now about being GLBTQ, but it's a good start. You'll read comments from experts in psychology, sociology, and health care. You'll get tips from people in national GLBTQ organizations. You'll also hear the true stories of teens and young adults who've been through some of the same things you might be facing. Some of these stories may be very different from your own. Some might feel so right you think they're speaking directly to you. Whether you are very secure with your sexual orientation or gender identity or you're just starting to get some things straight (so to speak), there is something in this book for you.

When it comes to questions about being GLBTQ, there aren't a lot of cut-and-dry answers. Because every GLBTQ person is an individual, it's difficult to provide answers that are appropriate for everyone. Even in the GLBTQ community there isn't always agreement on details surrounding certain issues. This book offers commonly accepted answers, as well as suggestions for how you can find answers to your own questions.

This is a handbook—use it as you need it. You can read it cover to cover, or use the contents and index to guide you to the chapters that feel right for your situation. You might be at a very different place in your life from another reader, so read the chapters you're ready for. This book is a pressure-free zone. The goal isn't to come up with definitive answers, because some answers might lead to other questions. And that's great. It's all part of getting to know yourself.

Even if you're just questioning or curious, that's okay, too. In fact, you never have to pick a label for yourself if you don't want to. Many people choose to identify themselves as "queer," or some even say "I don't identify. I just am who I am." You may decide you're just questioning right now. The purpose of this book is not to make you choose a definitive label, but instead to help you get to know yourself and be more comfortable with whoever that may be.

As you become more comfortable in your own skin, you'll soon learn that GLBTQ people come in all shapes, sizes, and colors: We are African American, Latino, Caucasian, Native American, Asian, and Indian. We are Catholic, Protestant, atheist, Buddhist, agnostic, Unitarian, Hindu, and Muslim. We can be teachers, lawyers, doctors, construction workers, executives, athletes, artists, writers, politicians, and any other career you can imagine. And we are parents, friends, partners, sons, daughters, sisters, brothers, aunts, uncles, and even grandparents. GLBTQ people are everywhere, and we can be anything we want to be.

1 GLBTQ 101

We are everywhere.

Maybe you've known you're GLBTQ for years. Or maybe you're only now beginning to question your sexual orientation or gender identity. Either way, you're not alone. Researchers believe that between five and six percent of youth are gay, lesbian, or bisexual. According to the 2000 U.S. Census, there are over 49 million school-age kids in America. That means there are over two and a half million kids just like you in America alone. Two and a half million!

Widely accepted research concludes that roughly one in ten adults is GLBTQ. Think about that the next time you're at the movies or a baseball game. Whether you're aware of them or not, it's a good chance that someone at your school or in your neighborhood is GLBTQ.

Yet differences in sexuality is a topic that a lot of people are uncomfortable talking about. You've probably grown up hearing a lot of rumors and myths about GLBTQ people. Even the most well-intentioned people can be misinformed about what it's like or what it means to be GLBTQ.

The most powerful response to bias and ignorance is knowledge. This chapter covers the fundamentals of being GLBTQ. Some of what follows may seem like very basic information, but even if you consider yourself knowledgeable about GLBTQ issues, you'll probably be surprised by some of the things you'll learn.

RESOURCE

If You Need Help Now

If you're feeling depressed or confused, or just want to talk to someone right now, pick up the phone and call the Trevor Helpline at 1-866-488-7386. The Trevor Helpline is a phone bank staffed by trained counselors who can talk to you about being a GLBTQ teen. The call is free and won't appear on your phone bill. Lines are open 24 hours a day, seven days a week, 365 days a year.

GLBTQ Basics

One thing that can be confusing about the GLBTQ community is the terminology. Sometimes it seems like a whole different language exists for queer people. Even among the GLBTQ population there is a lack of consensus about which words to use when, and even about definitions.

A few years ago, it was common to say "G&L" for gay and lesbian. But language evolves as our understanding of GLBTQ people evolves. When the "B" was added (for bisexual) the acronym became "GLB" or "LGB." Then "T" (for transgender) and "Q" (for questioning) joined the party. What was once G&L is now GLBTQ (though you might see these letters appear in a different order depending on the source).

In this book, you'll see the consistent use of the acronym GLBTQ. When an issue applies specifically to gay, lesbian, bisexual, or transgender people, those specific words will be used. And though you'll read about people being either GLBTQ or straight, not all transgender people are gay, lesbian, or bisexual. In fact, many transgender people are heterosexual. Referring to trans people as GLBTQ doesn't imply that they are necessarily gay, lesbian, or bisexual in their sexual orientation. The full acronym GLBTQ is used for consistency.

Another word used often in this book is "queer." This word was once used negatively to describe GLBTQ people. Now, many GLBTQ people (and others) use it in a very positive way. For example, you can find "Queer Studies" and "Queer Theory" courses at many colleges. The word "queer" is used in this book in a positive and affirming way. Queer is also a great word because it frees you from using a more specific label if you don't want to.

The back of the book has a full glossary of all the GLBTQ terms used in this book (and some you might come across elsewhere), but for now let's look at the essentials.

G is for Gay

This term is often used to describe both homosexual men and lesbians. As it refers to men, gay describes men who are physically and emotionally attracted to other men. The word "gay" didn't come into wide use to describe homosexual people until around the 1950s.

L is for Lesbian

Lesbians are women who are physically and emotionally attracted to other women. The word "lesbian" has its origins with the Greek poet Sappho, who was born some time between 630 and 612 B.C. For part of her life, Sappho lived on the island of Lesbos. Many of her poems dealt with same-sex love between women, and as a result, the island's name became synonymous with homosexual women and the word "lesbian" was born.

The Roots of Queer Language

According to *Hidden from History: Reclaiming the Gay & Lesbian Past,* by the late 1800s, lesbians who dressed and "passed" as men had developed a more positive language to describe themselves. While others used words such as "inverts," and "he-shes" to identify them, these women began to use words like "dike." At the time, the term referred to a man who was dressed up or "diked out" for a night on the town.

B is for Bisexual

Bisexuals are people who can be emotionally and physically attracted to people of either sex. Sometimes people refer to themselves as bisexual as a means of identifying themselves as questioning, or they identify as bisexual and then later identify as gay or lesbian. However, many bisexual people are bisexual, period, and that is what they will remain.

T is for Transgender

Transgender people have feelings of being a different gender from their physical anatomies. What it means to be transgender is complicated and often misunderstood. One misconception is that all transgender people want to have surgery and/or take hormones to change their bodies. Some do, others don't. Another misconception is that transgender people are all homosexual. Transgender people are often straight, but just like everyone else they can be gay, lesbian, or bisexual.

Some of the issues and emotions that transgender people may face are similar to those that gay, lesbian, and bisexual people experience. Feelings such as isolation and processes such as coming out, for example, are some of the things that all GLBTQ people may experience. However, there are other feelings and considerations that can come with identifying as the opposite physical gender. These issues are addressed in chapter 10.

Q is for Questioning

People who are questioning are uncertain of their sexual orientation or gender identity. Many teens are starting to be more comfortable identifying as questioning. A lot of things are changing during adolescence, and deciding you are questioning takes the pressure off of immediately choosing a label like gay, lesbian, bisexual, or straight.

A Biology Lesson? The Science of GLBTQ

You may be wondering why some people are GLBTQ and some aren't. There isn't a definitive answer. Scientists, philosophers, psychologists, and a host of others have offered opinions and theories to answer the question, but for now, there isn't a 100 percent proof-positive reason. There has, however, been a lot of research attempting to answer the question of what makes people GLBTQ. Thanks to these efforts, scientists, health care professionals, and the general public have access to expanded information on sexual orientation and gender identity.

The Kinsey Report

Don't worry. It's not a report you have to write. Instead of causing stress, this report might actually relieve some. In the 1940s, a scientist named Dr. Alfred Kinsey and his team of researchers conducted a study of human sexuality in men. Based on this research, Kinsey determined that most men are neither completely gay nor completely straight. (Kinsey was so intrigued by his research on male sexuality that he expanded his later work to include women, too.) Instead, while some people are at either end of the spectrum, most fall somewhere in the middle. He developed a six-point scale, the Kinsey Scale, to illustrate this spectrum.

Sexual Orientation: The Kinsey Scale

0 - Exclusively heterosexual

1 - Predominantly heterosexual, only incidentally homosexual

2 - Predominantly heterosexual, but more than incidentally homosexual

3 - Equally heterosexual and homosexual

4 - Predominantly homosexual, but more than incidentally heterosexual

5 - Predominantly homosexual, only incidentally heterosexual

6 - Exclusively homosexual

The Kinsey Scale was revolutionary not only because it looked at queerness as predetermined, but also because it showed there is a vast gray area between GLBTQ and straight. Before Kinsey, many experts thought it was black and white—straight people were 100 percent straight and queer people were 100 percent queer. Many also thought that straight people were "normal" and "well-adjusted," while queer people were "sick" or "deviant." Though the statistical methods Kinsey used to conduct his study fall short of the standards used for research today, thanks to Kinsey, there is strong evidence that people fall on a continuum of sexuality. While some people fall on points 6 or 0, most fall at one of the numbers in between.

If you've never thought of sexuality on a spectrum, the idea can be confusing. But if you think about all of the complex factors that contribute to making a single human being, it makes a little more sense. Everything human is on a spectrum. Some people are physically stronger or better at math or telling jokes. And even within a single quality there can be great variety. Take eye color, for example. A person with blue eyes can have light blue eyes, or deep blue eyes, or gray-blue eyes. Being human means being varied.

Maybe you're attracted to either girls or guys exclusively. Maybe you're usually attracted to boys, but there's something about that girl in your chemistry class that intrigues you. Or maybe at the last home-coming game you spent just as much time looking at the cheerlead-ers as the football players. All of these responses are natural.

> **BEEN THERE**
> "In my mind there was double the confusion—I liked half the guys in my senior class but also had a crush on two girls on my block. That's major confusion at an age when you are changing physically and mentally."—Enrique, 20*

Why Are People Queer or Straight?

That's the million dollar question. Over the course of your life you'll hear a lot of theories about why some people are GLBTQ and others aren't. There are queer people who believe you can choose to be GLBTQ. There are straight people who believe that you can't. Some say it's like putting on a suit that you can take off at any time. Others believe that it's something deep inside you. You might even hear someone joke about how an experience "made" someone gay. You might find that everyone has a theory about it, and you might even develop your own.

While some scientists are working to uncover a genetic compo-nent that makes people queer, most mental health professionals and GLBTQ activist and social concerns groups say that being GLBTQ is most likely the result of a complex interaction of environmental and bio-logical factors. The American Psychiatric Association and activist groups such as PFLAG say that being queer is not a choice. The American Psychological Association maintains unequivocally that "human beings cannot choose to be either gay or straight." In its pam-phlet *Answers to Your Questions About Sexual Orientation and Homosexuality* it states, "Although we can choose whether or not to act on our feelings, psychologists do not consider sexual orientation to be a conscious choice that can be voluntarily changed."

---

* The names of the teens and young adults quoted throughout the book have been changed to protect their privacy.

BEEN THERE

"I tell other GLBTQ teens that it's not your fault. You didn't do anything wrong. I know you feel strange and alone, but in reality there are so many people in your same situation at this very moment. Feeling this way is normal. Keep telling yourself that until you really believe it."—Sonia, 19

Wanting to Change and People Who Want to Change You

There are many stages of coming to terms with being GLBTQ. Early in that process, many teens wish they could change. Some ignore their feelings and try to act as if they are straight—going on dates, having romantic relationships, or sometimes even having sex.

Many of the people who have gone on to become leaders in the GLBTQ community started out just as confused and scared as you might be. Transgender activist and writer Kate Bornstein, who was born with male anatomy but always felt like a female, writes in her book *Gender Outlaw: On Men, Women, and the Rest of Us* about her experience of trying to hide her feelings of being a girl. "I knew from age four on that something was wrong with me being a guy, and I spent most of my life avoiding the issue," she writes. "I hid out in textbooks, pulp fiction, and drugs and alcohol. I buried my head in the sands of television, college, a lot of lovers, and three marriages." Bornstein eventually stopped trying to hide and grew to love and appreciate her true identity.

Overwhelmingly, medical and professional groups maintain that there is nothing wrong with being queer and that no one should attempt a "cure." In fact, the American Academy of Pediatrics, the American Counseling Association, the American Psychiatric Association, the National Association of School Psychologists, and the National Association of Social Workers, which together represent nearly half a million health and mental health professionals, all maintain that queerness is not a mental disorder.

However, there are some people who believe that you can change your gender identity or sexual orientation through therapy or other means. So-called "reparative therapy" or "transformational ministries" try to change or "cure" GLBTQ people. Reparative therapy, which is sometimes called "conversion therapy," involves psychotherapy aimed at eliminating feelings of homosexuality. Transformational ministries use religion to try to change people. Groups like Exodus International try to "free" people from being queer by pointing them toward God.

Reparative therapy and transformational ministries can be very destructive to queer people's self-esteem because their goal is to convince people that being GLBTQ is wrong or unnatural. If you need help coming to terms with being GLBTQ, or if you just want someone to talk to, seeking therapy or counseling to discuss these issues is a good idea. But you don't need to try to fix who you are because there is nothing wrong with you in the first place. In its *Guidelines for Psychotherapy with Lesbian, Gay, and Bisexual Clients*, the American Psychological Association states that being gay or bisexual is not a mental illness. Additionally, in 1998, the American Psychiatric Association issued a statement condemning reparative therapies, stating that attempts to transform gay or bisexual people into heterosexual people are pointless and are often motivated by personal prejudices.

RESOURCE

Ex-Gays

The Human Rights Campaign (HRC) offers materials on the so-called ex-gay movement. *Mission Impossible: Why Reparative Therapy and Ex-Gay Ministries Fail* and *Finally Free: How Love and Acceptance Saved Us from the Ex-Gay Ministries* both address this issue. Contact HRC by calling 1-800-777-4723 or visit *www.hrc.org*.

BEEN THERE

"When I first started to understand myself and tried to accept who I was, I was devastated. I remember a day when I took out my student Bible and searched for hours on homosexuality. When I finally found it, I was sobbing so hard I could barely breathe. There were a couple of passages that I thought were scolding me. They told me I was evil and hateful, that my kind is unforgiving and will forever burn. It was the harshest thing I had ever read. I probably prayed more within that week than I had ever prayed in my life. I begged for God to tell me if I was wrong and evil. I cried to myself, trying to get myself to believe that I'm not what they say I am. It took me a while to pull through that."—Sonia, 19

Your Personal Geography:
Exploring Who You Are

What it all boils down to is that it doesn't really matter what the experts say. What matters is what *you* say. You're the only person who can make a definitive statement about who you are. You can't control whether you're GLBTQ, but you can control how you feel about yourself. You have the power to improve your self-esteem.

Yes, No, Maybe So: It's Okay to Be Questioning

There's a line in the movie *Bring It On* when one of the female cheerleaders asks a male cheerleader if he's gay.

The boy just smiles and responds, "I'm . . . controversial."

Even if few (or no) people talk about it, questioning your sexual orientation is more common than you might think. A 1991 survey of junior and senior high school students conducted by the University of Minnesota Adolescent Health Project revealed that, although 88 percent described themselves as predominantly heterosexual and one percent said they were either bisexual or predominantly homosexual, over 10 percent reported being unsure of their sexual orientation. Though only one percent of students self-identified as homosexual, five percent reported having engaged in same-sex sexual activity.

Additionally, when asked about their fantasies, 6.5 percent of high school seniors reported that they were attracted primarily to people of the same sex.

> **BEEN THERE**
>
> **"If you are questioning, that doesn't necessarily mean that you're gay. It means exactly what it implies: you are questioning and unsure of yourself or your sexuality. In time, you will understand who you are."—Sonia, 19**

What's the Rush?

According to Caitlin Ryan and Donna Futterman, authors of *Lesbian & Gay Youth: Care & Counseling,* boys are often first aware of homosexual attractions by age 13, but often don't self-identify as gay until roughly age 19 to 21. On average, girls are first aware of homosexual attractions by age 14 to 16, but don't self-identify as lesbian until roughly age 21 to 23. These are averages. You don't have to fall into these age ranges. The point is, understanding your sexuality is a long process.

Figuring It Out: Three Teen Perspectives

Feelings about realizing you're GLBTQ are as varied as people's individual personalities. There's no "normal" way to react, and some know, or at least have an idea, earlier than others. The following stories show three people's reactions to suspecting or learning that they're GLBTQ.

> **"I realized I was GLBTQ when I was young, like 11 or 12. I always had an interest in the female sex, ever since I can remember. I distinctly remember watching television and 'liking' the pretty woman on the screen and wanting to touch her. I thought it was normal and didn't really think anything of it until I was 16 and I finally came out to myself."—Elena, 20**
>
> *continued* ⟶

"It's hard to say definitively how I became aware of my gender identity. I think it was really while I was surfing the Web sites and reading stories about [transgender] people that I realized not all guys
had dreams of suddenly and inexplicably being changed into a girl."
—Chris, 19

"I think I've known all my life that I am bisexual, even though I
didn't have a word for it then. I can remember playing with another
little girl when I was young, seven or eight maybe, and we'd play
'boyfriend' and 'girlfriend.' I have always been attracted to boys and
girls, but it wasn't until a friend of mine came out and told me he
was gay that I started thinking that I was."—June, 19

Common Feelings When You're Awakening

Although everyone reacts differently to the idea that he might be
GLBTQ, there is a very common progression of stages that people
usually go through. Some go through this process more quickly than
others, and many people spend a lot more time in one stage than
another. Sociologist Richard Troiden described the process in a 1988
article in the *Journal of Homosexuality* as follows:

Stage One: Sensitization

Feelings of being different from others in a fundamental way can
begin well before puberty. This is a very challenging time and can
make you feel isolated from your family and friends.

Stage Two: Identity confusion

This is when you start becoming aware of actual same-sex thoughts
and feelings. During this stage, learned negative thoughts about
homosexuality can make you feel betrayed by your own thoughts and
feelings.

Stage Three: Identity assumption

Things start getting a little better in this stage, which is when people begin to get more positive, accurate information about what it means to be GLBTQ and start to identify that way.

Stage Four: Commitment

Historically, people often didn't reach this final stage until adulthood, but these days more teens are reaching it. During this stage, people incorporate their sexual identity into all aspects of their lives, a big part of which is "coming out" to other people as GLBTQ.

> **BEEN THERE**
>
> "I came out to my sister and she was very weird about it, but things are becoming easier as I get older. I'm just becoming more comfortable with being bisexual."—Charlotte, 19
>
> "I came out to my family at the age of 15 as a lesbian. At the same time, I was questioning whether I was really a boy or a girl. Many times I would let the issue go and then come back to it. Finally, at 25, I was ready to really try to figure it out."—Lee, 26

What's Your (Stereo)type?
Myths, Generalizations, and Just Plain Silly Ideas About GLBTQ People . . . and the Truth

School is a hotbed of stereotypes. Based on how people dress or what they like to do after class, individuals get pigeonholed into categories like jock, geek, slacker, cheerleader, and so on. You've probably noticed that the problem with these labels is that they miss the whole person. You may dress like an athlete but have the soul of an artist, and vice versa.

The more you get to know someone, the less useful labels seem. Try describing your closest friend in a one-word stereotype. You'll find that a single word doesn't do her or him justice.

GLBTQ people are especially susceptible to stereotyping. One reason is that some people are afraid to challenge GLBTQ stereotypes because others might think they're GLBTQ, and then they might be harassed. Another reason is the lack of visibility—positive and accurate portrayals of GLBTQ people in the media have been rare.

Also, many GLBTQ people are afraid to come out because they fear rejection or even physical harm. The lack of an accepting environment keeps some GLBTQ people in hiding, which allows misinformation to thrive.

Fortunately, things are starting to change. GLBTQ activism is opening people's eyes to the truth and the media is showing gays more as everyday people (think of the television show *Will & Grace*).

Still, ignorance persists. For example, take the following ten GLBTQ stereotypes. You might have heard some, or all, of these ideas or statements.

Ten Absolutely Ridiculous Queer Stereotypes (and the Truth)

Myth #1: GLBTQ people are unhappy being who they are.

The truth: For a long time, society has painted a picture of GLBTQ people as living secretive or tormented lives. In reality, lots of GLBTQ people live open and happy lives. And just being straight doesn't guarantee that you'll have a great life, either. For both GLBTQ and straight people, life is what you make it.

Myth #2: Gay men find every man attractive, lesbians find every woman attractive, and bisexual people are attracted to just plain everyone.

The truth: Just like straight people, queer people have personal tastes in what they like, whether it's food, cars, or people they might want to date. This is a very common stereotype and one that can make some people uncomfortable when you first meet them. But there's a big difference between coming out to someone and coming on to them.

Myth #3: Gay men want to be women and lesbians want to be men.

The truth: Being transgender and being gay or lesbian are very different things. Some people have such a hard time understanding same-sex attractions that they assume that gay men and women actually want to be the opposite physical sex. This stereotype also has roots in how some gay men and lesbians challenge gender norms. Gay men who are seen as more *femme* (a term used to describe both males and females who act and dress in stereotypically feminine ways) and lesbians who dress or act more *butch* (a term used to describe both males and females who act and dress in stereotypically masculine ways) are often assumed to want to change their genders.

Myth #4: Bisexual people are gay men and lesbians in denial.

The truth: Unfortunately, bisexual people are sometimes discriminated against by both straight people and queer people. Bisexual people are just that, and deserve to have their feelings respected just like everyone else, queer or straight. It's true that some people identify as bisexual for a time before realizing they are gay or lesbian, but many people are bisexual, period.

Myth #5: Transgender people are all drag queens and drag kings.

The truth: Drag queens are men who dress as women and perform for entertainment and drag kings are women who dress as men and perform for entertainment. Transgender people have a deep, personal identification with a gender that is different from their anatomy. Transgender people don't dress or act certain ways to get attention or for entertainment, but instead to reflect who they are inside. Some transgender people are also drag queens or kings, but many are not.

Myth #6: GLBTQ people are only into partying and drugs.

The truth: For a long time, some of the only safe places for GLBTQ people to get together were in queer or queer-friendly bars and clubs. They became not only places to socialize, but also, in some cases, places to meet and organize civil rights efforts. The club and bar scenes are still popular today, but GLBTQ people socialize in other places, as well. Just like straight people, queer people have a variety of interests.

Myth #7: All gay men are interior decorators or hairdressers and lesbians are all construction workers or prison guards.

The truth: Some of us are, and that's great, but many of us aren't. Look at fashion model Jenny Shimizu. She's a lesbian. And how about gay former professional football player Esera Tuaolo? Not only are we everywhere, but we're in every imaginable profession.

Myth #8: Queer people can't be parents.

Many queer people have children. Some GLBTQ people adopt, some have children from previous marriages, some undergo artificial insemination or use a surrogate mother. It used to be that a "normal" family was nuclear—a mom, dad, and two kids. Today, there might be two moms or two dads. Or maybe even a mom and two dads, or two moms and two dads.

Myth #9: Queer people only live in urban areas.

The truth: There's a bumper sticker that reads "We're everywhere." That's no joke. By many commonly accepted estimates, as many as one in ten people are GLBTQ. It's easy to feel alone when you first realize you're GLBTQ, but you aren't. Not by a long shot. There is even a Web site with resources for queer teens in rural areas— *www.youthresource.com/ourlives/rural/index.cfm.*

Myth #10: Gay men can't commit to a long-term relationship and lesbians can't not commit.

The truth: This plays on the idea that men like to date around while women want to be in relationships. Much of this is based more on stereotypes about gender than about GLBTQ men and women. Men have gotten the reputation of being unable to commit and women are often thought of as wanting to settle down. The truth is, these are just generalizations, and there are many happy gay male couples and plenty of single lesbians.

Your Own Beliefs About GLBTQ People

Some of the most difficult GLBTQ stereotypes to conquer can be the ones you hold yourself. You might not realize it, but you could believe some inaccurate information about GLBTQ people. By adolescence, most teens have internalized at least some negative messages they've received about GLBTQ people.

Stereotypes about GLBTQ people can also make it tough to know that you're queer. Some people say they had trouble figuring out that they were GLBTQ because they didn't seem to fit the "definition" of what that meant. But it turns out that definition was based on stereotypes, and what it means to be GLBTQ is different for each person.

Out comedian Elvira Kurt has a bit half-way into in her stand-up routine when she comes out to the audience, then teases them about their shocked reactions. "Well, she has the short hair, but she's wearing a dress and lipstick. Is she butch or femme?" she jokes. She laughs and explains that she is part of a vast space between butch and femme that she likes to call "fellagirly."

Some GLBTQ people adhere to some of the same stereotypes about queer people that straight people do. Maybe you think that because you're GLBTQ, you won't be able to pursue your chosen profession or have children. Maybe you think it means you'll have to dress or act a certain way to attract other GLBTQ people. But that's not true. The GLBTQ community is as rich and diverse as the straight community, and there's plenty of room for you just as you are.

Check Your Head

It can be difficult to face negative stereotypes, especially when you apply them to yourself. Here are some thoughts to help you unlearn some of the negative misinformation that could be affecting how you feel about yourself. If you're struggling, repeat them to yourself. The more you do, the more you'll start to believe them.

1. I am a human being who happens to be GLBTQ. It isn't all that I am, but it is a part of me and a part that I embrace.

2. Being GLBTQ means only that—it's my sexual orientation/gender identity. I can be anything I want to be.

3. I am my own person. I can wear what I want, say what I want, and do what I want.

Some Famous Queer People from Yesterday and Today

If you're still not convinced, look at this list. GLBTQ people have always existed. Throughout history and into today, GLBTQ people can be found in all walks of life, including some rather surprising places. The following list is a sampling of people from yesterday and today who were or are gay, lesbian, bisexual, or transgender.

Edward Albee (playwright)

Alexander the Great (Macedonian ruler)

Pedro Almodóvar (director)

W.H. Auden (writer)

Sir Francis Bacon (writer)

Joan Baez (musician)

Josephine Baker (musician)

James Baldwin (writer)

Tammy Baldwin (politician)

Alan Ball (Oscar-winning screenwriter)

Clive Barker (writer)

Deborah Batts (federal judge)

Amanda Bearse (actress)

Andy Bell (musician)

Ruth Benedict (anthropologist)

Michael Bennett (choreographer)

Sandra Bernhard (comedian)

Kate Bornstein (writer/ performance artist)

David Bowie (musician)

Rev. Malcolm Boyd (Episcopal priest)

Boy George (musician)

continued⟶

Benjamin Britten (composer)

Rita Mae Brown (writer)

Glenn Burke (professional baseball player)

Frank Buttino (former FBI agent)

Lord Byron (poet)

Julius Caesar (emperor)

Margarethe Cammermeyer (former National Guard Colonel)

Willa Cather (writer)

Margaret Cho (comedian)

Peter Christopherson (musician)

Jean Cocteau (artist)

Colette (writer)

Aaron Copland (composer)

Chief Crazy Horse (Sioux chief)

George Cukor (movie director)

Alan Cumming (actor)

James Dean (actor)

Ellen DeGeneres (actor/comedian)

Lea DeLaria (comedian)

Ramon Escobar (television executive)

Melissa Etheridge (musician)

Rupert Everett (actor)

Leslie Feinberg (writer/activist)

Harvey Fierstein (actor/playwright)

Will Fitzpatrick (politician)

Errol Flynn (actor)

E.M. Forster (writer)

Barney Frank (politician)

Frederick the Great (emperor)

Rudy Galindo (Olympic figure skater)

David Geffen (music producer)

Sir John Gielgud (actor)

Tim Gill (founder of Quark Inc.)

Allen Ginsberg (poet)

Rob Halford (musician)

Lorraine Hansberry (playwright)

Bruce Hayes (Olympic swimmer)

David Hockney (artist)

Janis Ian (musician)

Indigo Girls (musicians)

Bob Jackson-Paris (professional body-builder)

Marc Jacobs (fashion designer)

Henry James (writer)

King James I of England (who was also King James VI of Scotland)

Elton John (musician)

Jasper Johns (artist)

Frieda Kahlo (artist)

David Kopay (professional football player)

Tony Kushner (playwright)

Dave LaChapelle (photographer)

Nathan Lane (actor)

k.d. lang (musician)

Fran Lebowitz (writer)

Simon LeVay (biologist)

Frederico García Lorca (poet)

Greg Louganis (Olympic diver)

Amy Lowell (poet)

W. Somerset Maugham (writer)

Amélie Mauresmo (tennis player)

Sir Ian McKellen (actor)

John J. McNeill (religious scholar)

Keith Meinhold (Navy officer)

continued ⟶

Stephin Merritt (musician)

Nathan Meunier (rapper)

Michelangelo (artist)

Edna St. Vincent Millay (poet)

Yukio Mishima (writer)

Bob Mould (musician)

Megan Mullally (actor)

Martina Navratilova (professional tennis player)

Meshell Ndegéocello (musician)

Rosie O'Donnell (actor/comedian)

Georgia O'Keeffe (artist)

Todd Oldham (fashion designer)

Dave Pallone (former professional baseball umpire)

Pet Shop Boys (musicians)

Phranc (musician)

Plato (philosopher)

Deb Price (syndicated newspaper columnist)

Marcel Proust (writer)

Christopher Rice (writer)

Dr. Renée Richards (professional tennis player)

Eleanor Roosevelt (former First Lady)

RuPaul (actor/entertainer)

Yves Saint Laurent (fashion designer)

Sappho (poet)

Dick Sargent (actor)

May Sarton (writer)

Kate Schellenbach (musician)

Franz Schubert (composer)

David Sedaris (writer)

Randy Shilts (journalist)

Bessie Smith (musician)

Liz Smith (gossip columnist)

Socrates (philosopher)

Jimmy Somerville (musician)

Stephen Sondheim (lyricist/composer)

Dusty Springfield (musician)

Joseph Steffan (Navy officer)

Gertrude Stein (writer)

Michael Stipe (musician)

Gerry Studds (politician)

Peter Tchaikovsky (composer)

Dorothy Thompson (journalist)

Scott Thompson (comedian/actor)

Alice B. Toklas (writer)

Lily Tomlin (actor)

Gus Van Sant (movie director)

Gore Vidal (writer)

Leonardo da Vinci (artist)

Tom Waddell (Olympic athlete)

Rufus Wainwright (musician)

Andy Warhol (artist)

John Waters (movie director)

Walt Whitman (writer)

Emil Wilbekin (magazine editor)

Oscar Wilde (writer)

Tennessee Williams (playwright)

Kevin Williamson (writer/producer)

Jeanette Winterson (writer)

B.D. Wong (actor)

Virginia Woolf (writer)

Wu (Chinese emperor)

Babe Didrikson Zaharias (professional golfer)

José Zuniga (former Army sergeant)

2 HOMOPHOBIA

Hate is not a family value.

Even though we know there have been GLBTQ people since the beginning of time, if you look at most history books, queer people are largely ignored. When GLBTQ people are acknowledged, they are often portrayed as immoral or unnatural. This combination of invisibility and misinformation has contributed to widespread ignorance regarding GLBTQ people. That ignorance often manifests itself as *homophobia*.

Homophobia can put a lot of pressure on you, especially at school. You may be comfortable with being GLBTQ, but your fellow students, your teachers, and even your friends might be uncomfortable. Some people can even be hateful and violent.

Homophobia can make you feel lousy—all you want to do is be yourself, but no one wants to let you. It can also inspire you to try to change the world. Either way, the absolute most important thing to remember is that *homophobia isn't about you*. It's about other people and their ignorance. Homophobia might cause you problems in your life, but it's not *your* problem. You didn't do anything to deserve it.

So where does homophobia come from, and if there's nothing wrong with GLBTQ people, why doesn't it just go away?

The 411 on Hate: The Roots of Homophobia

Homophobia is a negative emotion like fear, anger, or suspicion toward someone for being GLBTQ. It can also take the form of ignorance about GLBTQ people. Homophobia can be very overt, like someone shouting "dyke!" or "fag!" in the hall, or it can be more subtle, like a teammate quietly trying to avoid being near you in the locker room.

From Uncomfortable to Hateful: Shades of Homophobia

Although homophobia is never a good thing, it has degrees ranging from mild to severe. For example, people who are ignorant about what it means to be GLBTQ can change their negative ideas when they find out a friend or family member is GLBTQ. They begin to understand that we are human beings just like everyone else.

For others, homophobia is more deeply rooted and takes form as hatred of GLBTQ people. These people may act out in ways that range from lobbying to pass anti-queer legislation to physically hurting GLBTQ people. There are lots of homophobic people who would never dream of physically hurting another human being, but heartbreaking incidents like Matthew Shepard's brutal murder in 1998 show that a lot of hatred exists in this world. Such incidents mean that GLBTQ people need to think seriously about their safety.

What Makes People Homophobic?

The dictionary defines a phobia as an irrational fear. So, by definition, homophobia is not based on reason.

According to clinical psychologist Dr. Sandy Loiterstein, who works as a support group coordinator for the Metropolitan Washington D.C. chapter of PFLAG, homophobia can have a variety of sources. "One of these is the perception that being GLBTQ is a choice," she said in an interview. "Some people get very angry or frustrated with GLBTQ people because they don't understand why they would make such a choice. There's also an inability to see GLBTQ people as individuals. Instead they're seen through stereotypes. Ancient fears of differentness, probably the major source of homophobia, have been perpetuated by religious and other institutions, including mental health organizations. As recently as 1976, the American Psychiatric Association finally removed their classification of homosexuality as a mental illness."

In some cases, the historic roots of anti-GLBTQ sentiment really don't have much to do with being queer. In some cultures, any sexual contact between two people that could not result in the conception of a child, such as oral sex, was considered sinful or morally wrong regardless of whether it was between people of different sexes or the same one. In some cases, it was the act rather than the biological sex of the people engaged in it that was frowned upon. According to *Hidden from History: Reclaiming the Gay & Lesbian Past,* some historians believe that in certain cultures and religions the roots of homophobia extend back to such beliefs.

Common Fears About GLBTQ People

Rhonda Buckner, Executive Director of the Metropolitan Washington D.C. chapter of PFLAG identified some common fears and misconceptions about queer people.

1. Being GLBTQ automatically means you're attracted to *everyone* of the same sex, or, for bisexuals, everyone.

2. Being GLBTQ is not normal or natural.

3. If someone is supportive of you, they are either GLBTQ themselves or people will perceive them to be.

4. GLBTQ people try to "recruit" or influence others to "become" GLBTQ.

5. GLBTQ people and straight people have little to nothing in common.

Some Negative Images of GLBTQ People in Movies

Hollywood is famous for playing on people's fears of GLBTQ people. *The Celluloid Closet: Homosexuality in the Movies* by Vito Russo explores the history of GLBTQ people in film. He discusses how the portrayal of GLBTQ people in Hollywood films has run the gamut from invisibility (nope, no queers here) to homophobic stereotypes (queer people are silly or scary). From sissies to psychotic killers, you may be surprised at how long the negative stereotypes about queer people you still see in films today have been around.

GLBTQ People Can Be Homophobic, Too

Another kind of homophobia is *internalized homophobia.* People with internalized homophobia have difficulty accepting that they are GLBTQ. They feel guilty about who they are or feel that being queer means there is something wrong with them.

George Weinberg, the psychologist and GLBTQ rights activist who coined the terms homophobia and internalized homophobia, stated in a 2002 interview in the magazine *Gay Today* that internalized homophobia is the fear of being different, of being singled out, punished, or laughed at. Weinberg explained that internalized homophobia decreases as people are able to accept themselves for who they are, regardless of what others might think.

Invisibility as Homophobia

When you're GLBTQ, sometimes you wish people would just stop acting like it's a huge deal. Conversely, there are situations when queer people might seem nonexistent. For example, if you're a girl, it can be frustrating, embarrassing, or nerve-racking when relatives or others continually ask, "Do you have a boyfriend yet?" instead of asking something that makes fewer assumptions such as, "Are you dating anyone special?"

That kind of question is a good example of *heterosexism.* Heterosexism is the idea that heterosexual people are the norm and that GLBTQ people are somehow abnormal. It is the assumption that people are heterosexual that contributes to homophobia.

The Big Bad World?
Homophobia in Society and at School

Have you ever heard of *mob mentality?* It's when an individual might not normally do something, but because she sees other people doing it, she thinks it must be okay or feels pressure to join in.

One reason homophobia is so common is mob mentality. When a handful of people speak out strongly against GLBTQ people and their ideas go unchallenged, ignorance and hatred can persist.

How common is homophobia? Common enough that GLBTQ activists are fighting against it all over the world. In the United States, the Gay and Lesbian Alliance Against Defamation (GLAAD) is working to encourage positive, informed portrayals of GLBTQ people in the media. The Human Rights Campaign (HRC) and National Gay and Lesbian Task Force (NGLTF) are working to enact social change by getting legislation passed that protects GLBTQ people and their civil rights. Internationally, PFLAG is working to increase understanding of and support for GLBTQ people by changing attitudes about them. These are just some of the many groups working to make the world a better place for GLBTQ people.

Every day people are lobbying legislators to pass queer-friendly laws like the Employment Non-Discrimination Act (ENDA), which would prevent workplace discrimination based on sexual orientation. In 2000, California passed the California Student Safety and Violence Prevention Act. A student named George Loomis and a coalition of local groups, PFLAG, the American Civil Liberties Union (ACLU), and the Gay-Straight Alliance Network (GSA Network) used the law to bring a suit against Loomis's former school for allowing ongoing abuse and harassment. In 2002, they won, and as a result, the school district will have to initiate widespread antidiscrimination efforts.

Homophobia in the Hallways: Life at School

If you've ever been singled out verbally or physically because you're GLBTQ, you're not alone. A 1997 study of high school students in Iowa showed that students heard anti-GLBTQ slurs an average of 25 times per day. The 2001 Gay, Lesbian and Straight Education Network (GLSEN) National School Climate Survey found that 65 percent of GLBTQ students reported being sexually harassed, four in ten reported physical harassment, and 21 percent reported physical assault.

> **BEEN THERE**
> "When I was in 11th grade and being harassed constantly, the teacher was doing nothing. I never talked to her about it. I never asked her to stop anti-gay slurs, and I think that she should have."—Brian, 19

Currently there is a big debate about giving kids access to positive information about GLBTQ people. GLBTQ advocates claim that giving students positive and accurate information about GLBTQ issues will reduce harassment of students who are or who are perceived to be GLBTQ. Opponents claim that these efforts encourage and promote queerness.

Many groups, including GLSEN and PFLAG, have "safe schools" movements where adults and teens work together to make school environments safer for kids who are or who are perceived to be GLBTQ. GLSEN says its research shows that 83 percent of parents support putting in place or expanding existing antiharassment and antidiscrimination policies to include GLBTQ students.

It's a tough battle, but these efforts have resulted in real accomplishments. Some school boards have been persuaded to add sexual orientation and gender identity to their codes of conduct. That means students, faculty, and staff are barred from discriminating against others who are or who are perceived to be GLBTQ. These rules usually already include race, gender, religious affiliation, disability, and more.

Some schools sponsor assemblies to educate students about GLBTQ people, while others now allow gay pride month displays. Some students form gay-straight alliance clubs (GSAs) to educate others in their schools and work for change.

There is a large "safe schools" movement underway to help GLBTQ students feel safe and welcome at school. Still, if you're facing homophobia now, it might feel like it will be forever until things change at your school.

Take That! Responding to Homophobia

Understanding homophobia and where it comes from is one thing. Figuring out what you're going to do about it is another.

Prejudice can show itself in many ways. A GLBTQ teen might be cut from a sports team or dubbed a "troublemaker" by teachers. An administrator could turn a blind eye to harassment or tell a teen that he brought it on himself. There are a number of possible ways to react to such incidents, ranging from ignoring them to confronting the people involved.

How Homophobia Can Make You Feel

Dealing with homophobia can make you feel scared, isolated, depressed, and just plain worn out. Sometimes it may feel like fighting homophobia is an uphill battle, like things will never get better. Even if you feel comfortable about being GLBTQ and good about yourself overall, facing regular harassment can be demoralizing.

BEEN THERE

"Daily, more and more people would use those words—fag, homo, queer, sissy. Eventually things moved from not only words, but also to violence and pranks. The word 'faggot' was written on the locker next to mine because they made a mistake of which locker was mine. People put gum in my hair, stuck papers on my back, and threw things at me. There was physical violence, death threats. The school did 'the best they could do,' as they put it. In my mind, little was done."—Robert, 15

As you'll see in the sections that follow, you can address homophobia in many ways. Regardless of how you decide to handle it, it's important to remember that you're not to blame for the bad treatment you're receiving, and you're not alone in experiencing homophobia. Do activities that make you feel good about yourself. Writing, drawing, dancing, working out, or hanging out with friends are all great options. Take time to check in with yourself every so often to make sure that homophobia isn't taking a toll on your self-esteem.

Assessing the Situation

Safety needs to be your first concern. So, before you decide how to react to homophobia, assess the situation.

1. Is the person merely being ignorant? Or do they mean to do you some kind of harm?

2. Is the person aggressive with her words or body language? Is she threatening you, using a threatening tone, or moving closer to you?

3. Has this person harassed you before? If so, has there been an escalation in the harassment? (Perhaps a taunt in the hallway has turned into shoving or worse.)

4. Are you alone or do you have friends with you? Is there an adult nearby who could help?

5. Where are you? Can you get away?

Homophobia stirs up a lot of emotions. Even so, it's important to look at the situation rather than react based on your feelings. Maybe the girl in your class wasn't trying to be mean when she made that comment, she just didn't realize how it sounded. But the bully who throws stuff at you might become increasingly violent in the future.

Options for Responding

The first option is to turn the other cheek. That's hard to do, because encountering homophobia can be so frustrating. Sometimes what you really feel like doing is lashing out, but try to consider the most productive, effective, and safest ways to respond.

Some people use humor to help them turn the other cheek or to diffuse the situation. For example, when one woman, who is very out and open about being a lesbian, heard a man shout, "Dyke!" at her, she turned around and, without missing a beat, smiled and said, "Why, thank you!" His jaw dropped. Shocked and flustered, he just left.

You can also ignore homophobia completely by acting like you didn't hear the remark or by not reacting to the sign stuck on your backpack; instead just throw it away. But ignoring and forgiving homophobia is rarely an option if you're placed in a dangerous situation.

Speaking Up

Speaking up and talking back is another option. Again, consider the situation—talking back should be limited to situations when responding would be, or at least could be, productive. (Sometimes productivity means *you* feel better.) By keeping your wits about you, you can sometimes turn a negative situation into a more positive one by talking back when someone demonstrates his homophobia.

> **BEEN THERE**
>
> "When I was in tenth grade, a teacher mentioned something about there being gay students at our school and the girl I was sitting next to asked 'There are gay people in this school?' and the guy sitting next to her, the girl sitting in front of her, and I all turned and said 'yes' at the same time. By my twelfth-grade year, no one would ask that question."—Brian, 19

If you decide to respond to someone who is being homophobic, here are a few ground rules that will help encourage a positive result:

1. Don't match insult for insult. This will only escalate the situation.

2. Try to get the person to name her behavior by asking, in a nonconfrontational tone (if you can manage it), "Why would you say something like that?" or "Are you aware that sounds homophobic?" or something similar.

3. Make your responses about how the comments or actions make you feel instead of about the person who said them. Instead of saying, "You're only saying that because you're ignorant," try, "There are a lot of misconceptions about queer people. We're all human beings, and it can really hurt to hear those kinds of things."

4. If a person gets aggressive or threatening and you can't improve the situation, get yourself out of it as quickly and calmly as possible.

There may be times when it's appropriate just to turn around and say, "I really didn't appreciate that comment." However, if you're going to talk back, include something constructive. Tell the person why you don't appreciate his comments or how the comments or actions make you feel, but keep your cool while you're doing it. Homophobia is an issue that's easy to get upset about. A comment you intended to be constructive could escalate into a fight.

In the heat of the moment, it can be tough to think of something to say beyond four-letter words. Here are some common homophobic remarks along with possible responses. Some are humorous, some not, but all are designed to make people think about what they said:

When someone tells a homophobic joke.
Possible response: "When you tell jokes like that, you give the impression that it's okay to make fun of GLBTQ people. Is that what you really believe?"

"That is sooo gay."
Possible response: "Comments like that are sooo straight."

"He's such a fag."
Possible response: "How would you feel if I called you a 'breeder'?"

"So what do queer people do in bed?"
Possible response: "Sleep. Sometimes we watch TV or read."

"But you don't *look* gay."
Possible response: "That's because I'm one of our secret agents. Glad to know the disguise is working."

To a girl: "You just haven't met the right guy yet."
Possible response to another girl: "Okay, and maybe you just haven't met the right *girl* yet."

"You're just going through a phase."
Possible response: "Is my entire life a phase?"

"Gay people spread AIDS."
Possible response: "Actually, according to the National Institutes of Health, the fastest growing population of HIV positive people are heterosexual women."

"Why do gay people have to flaunt who they are?"
Possible response: "Refusing to hide is not flaunting."

"Gay people are disgusting."
Possible response: "Ignorance and hatred are disgusting."

Another option when you hear a homophobic remark or question is to name it. Say, "That comment is homophobic" or even ask "What is it about GLBTQ people that makes you so afraid?"

Try to Educate Others

Another option, which goes hand-in-hand with speaking up, is trying to turn the incident into an educational opportunity. You can address the roots of the homophobia by asking something like, "What is it you think about GLBTQ people that makes you say that?"

Realistically, this approach will be more effective with friends and acquaintances than with someone who is threatening to hurt you. Not everyone will be receptive, but even if someone doesn't react positively right away, down the road she might think about what you said and it might have a more lasting and positive effect.

Some people don't even realize that things they say are offensive. It can be particularly painful when a friend or family member makes negative comments or jokes about GLBTQ people. Some people ask questions that they wouldn't ask their straight friends, and that can be offensive, too.

Fighting Homophobia Through Activism

Like George Loomis and other teens who have taken formal action to end harassment and educate others, young people all over are working to create change on local and national levels. Eagle Scout Steven Cozza took on the entire Boy Scouts of America organization and is fighting to make them more accepting of gay Scouts. Steven's willingness to speak out about homophobia in scouting sparked a national movement and now his group, Scouting for All, has thousands of members who have helped bring major attention to the issue.

Teens are taking legal action to fight school harassment and bring it to national attention. In a 1999 law suit, a gay student in Wisconsin sued his school district for failing to protect him against repeated harassment in junior high and high school. The case resulted in a $900,000 award in favor of the student.

> **BEEN THERE**
> "One year we organized a National Coming Out Day event, which consisted of putting up posters and handing out rainbow stickers. It was great. There were rainbows all over the school, on many people's backpacks who I'd never even met! But best of all, people stopped using 'gay' as an all-purpose insult. When people started to realize that they knew gay people and that gay people were being affected by slurs, a lot of people stopped using them."—Brian, 19

Maybe you'll join or even start a GSA or other GLBTQ group. Maybe you'll get involved with a local or national organization. There are lots of options. Groups like GLSEN, GLAAD, and HRC, to name just a few, are always happy for more volunteers. They also can provide you with ideas about things you can do to help make your own area a more friendly place for queer people.

> **BEEN THERE**
> "I got involved with a group called Lambda . . . which had a speakers' bureau. We would go to high schools and middle schools and talk to students and teachers about our experiences coming out and answer questions that they had."—Sonia, 19

Getting involved and working for change not only has a positive result, but it also helps you feel better about yourself and the homophobia you might be facing. It can be depressing and frustrating to run up against ignorance, and it can often make you feel helpless. Getting involved helps you feel like you have the power to make a change in your world. It's also a great way to gain support and meet other GLBTQ and GLBTQ-friendly people.

Being an activist can be a very consuming experience. Be sure to make time for yourself, your schoolwork, your job, your friends, and any other positive things you have in your life.

BEEN THERE

"We have become part of the 'post-gay' era when some people just want to live their lives, maybe not even coming out . . . or not taking part in any activist events because they think they are boring, the events don't have anything to do with them, or they don't think anything will be accomplished. I'm not judging this attitude . . . but I feel that if we are not visible we will always be in the shadows. People won't notice our needs and the prejudice we still face. A bit of participation in a few events will show the world we are not afraid . . . even if we are."—Enrique, 20

When Homophobia Becomes Harassment

Sometimes, homophobia manifests itself in harassment. Not just a remark here or there (although those remarks can hurt), but constant badgering, escalating teasing, or physical threats. Harassment is not okay, and you do not have to live with it.

GLSEN advises students to document incidents of harassment. Write down who did or said what, when, and where. Note anyone who was there and witnessed the incident. And keep it all together in a file or notebook. That way when you report it, you have a written record of exactly what happened. This especially comes in handy if the person or people you tell fail to do anything about it.

So who do you tell about harassment? Telling an approachable teacher, counselor, or administrator are all options. Maybe one of your teachers or a school staff member has witnessed the harassment and will support you if you go to the administration.

It can be very daunting to approach an administrator. Not only are you upset about the incident or incidents, you're also worried about the administrator's reaction. It's even tougher if you aren't comfortable being GLBTQ or talking about it. For that reason, it's a good idea to get a parent or other adult to go with you. They can support you, and their presence can also help show the administrator that harassment is a serious matter and won't be tolerated.

Here are tips for approaching an administrator or other adult:

1. Stay calm. If you present your case in a calm, rational way, it will be harder for the adult to dismiss you as overreacting or being too emotional.

2. Provide an exact account, as detailed as you can remember, about what happened. It's also helpful if you have witnesses who are willing to back up your story.

3. Explain that your safety is in jeopardy as long as the issue continues unaddressed.

BEEN THERE

"Diversity in my community is bowling on Tuesdays instead of Saturdays. The majority of my attackers were never punished. On one occasion, three boys were suspended for three days. The principal told me they were suspended for the verbal attacks and not the physical one, as the physical one could not be proven. I had several witnesses report it to him, but he just didn't want to do much about it. Later, I was attacked in the hallway. I do not remember much of it, as my head was hit on the locker several times and I must have blacked out or something. After that, I got a lawyer through the ACLU (American Civil Liberties Union) and a couple of national organizations helped me and came in to the school to talk to them. The school has been very supportive recently. Maybe that was because of my influence and pressure on them."—Robert, 15

Some administrators will be outraged. Others will be extremely reluctant to take action. Some even imply or say outright that GLBTQ students invite harassment by being out. If you are assaulted (the legal definition is a threat of harm) or battered (physically attacked), you can file a report with the police. If no one will help you, you can reach out to a national organization like GLSEN or the National Gay and Lesbian Task Force (NGLTF). There might be a local group listed in your phone directory that can help you. Either way, you do not have to accept harassment, and you do not have to confront it alone.

RESOURCE

Help for Harassment

Gay, Lesbian and Straight Education Network (GLSEN)
(212) 727-0135
www.glsen.org
glsen@glsen.org

Human Rights Campaign (HRC)
(202) 628-4160
www.hrc.org

National Gay and Lesbian Task Force (NGLTF)
(202) 393-5177
www.thetaskforce.org
thetaskforce@thetaskforce.org

Parents, Families and Friends of Lesbians and Gays (PFLAG)
(202) 467-8180
www.pflag.org
info@pflag.org

To find your local American Civil Liberties Union (ACLU) chapter, visit *www.aclu.org* or look in your local telephone directory.

3 COMING OUT

We're here. We're queer. Get used to it.

Throughout history, GLBTQ people have often felt the need to hide who they are to avoid harassment and discrimination. A gradual shift in society's attitudes toward GLBTQ people has been occurring. This shift, combined with turning-point events like the 1969 Stonewall riot (when a group of GLBTQ people stood up to police harassment in June), has helped create an atmosphere where more people feel comfortable coming out. (Commemorations of the Stonewall riot eventually became the GLBTQ pride parades that take place every June.) Many GLBTQ people used to hide their identities, but today, more and more are open about who they are.

Coming out, on one level, is very simple. It's nothing more than being open with family, friends, and others about identifying as

GLBTQ. On another level, coming out or being out isn't so simple. It can expose you to everything from awkward social situations, such as people trying to fix you up with the only other GLBTQ person they know, to prejudice and even harassment.

> **BEEN THERE**
>
> "As a freshman in college I came out to a friend of mine. At first, I thought it might be a big mistake because she was the most popular freshman on campus. But I thought that since she trusted me with her deepest secrets, then I could trust her with mine. When I told her she said, 'Wow, that's cool. You know, I didn't want to ask but . . .' That was the beginning of our friendship on a whole new level."—Elena, 20

The decision to come out is a significant one, especially when you're a teen. Some teens who come out are harassed and experience violence at home or at school. Some teens are kicked out of the house or are forced to run away. These things don't happen to everyone, but it's important to seriously consider your safety and well-being before coming out.

But there are many positive aspects about coming out. You can live your life openly and meet other GLBTQ people. Many GLBTQ teens say being out feels liberating. It can be very empowering to be honest about who you are.

The purpose of this chapter is not to tell you whether or not you should come out—it's to help you decide what's right for you. Even if you don't feel like you have a lot of control over your life, *you* are the only person who can ultimately decide how to live *your* life, and that includes making decisions about how out you want to be. If you do decide to come out, this chapter will give you some advice on how best to do it.

What Is Coming Out All About?

As you learn more about the GLBTQ community, you'll find that coming out is a very meaningful issue. Some people will ask you if you're out, or who you're out to, or they'll want to share their coming-out stories. Sometimes it seems like everybody who is GLBTQ is obsessed with the idea of being out. There is a GLBTQ magazine called *Out*; Frank DeCaro, the movie critic for *The Daily Show with Jon Stewart*, does a segment called "Out at the Movies"; and there is even a National Coming Out Project.

RESOURCE

The National Coming Out Project

The Human Rights Campaign (HRC)—a group dedicated to working for GLBTQ civil rights—sponsors the National Coming Out Project, which is designed to promote openness about being GLBTQ. The HRC Web site includes some great information about the project and also about coming out in general. To learn more, visit *www.hrc.org* or call HRC at (202) 628-4160, (This is a toll call outside of the Washington, D.C., area.)

Coming out is the process of telling others that you are GLBTQ. The phrase "coming out" comes from the metaphor that you are "coming out of the closet." Conversely, people who are not out are often referred to as being "closeted," meaning they've chosen not to tell others of their GLBTQ identity.

There's a whole range of being out. People can be completely out, meaning they're open with everyone about being GLBTQ. Others are partially out, meaning they're out to some people but not others. Others might only be out to one very close person in their lives. Some people are not out at all.

Queer in the Military

During World War II, if military personnel were discovered to be GLBTQ, they were often given special dishonorable discharges. These were called "blue discharges" because the form on which they were typed was blue. People who received blue discharges

continued——➤

often had trouble finding employment and faced rejection in civilian life. Today, the military holds a "Don't Ask, Don't Tell" policy that forbids officials from inquiring about sexual orientation or gender identity, but allows them to discharge GLBTQ personnel if they are discovered. As a result, GLBTQ people in military service are still forced to hide their sexual orientations and gender identities. Groups like the Servicemembers Legal Defense Network are working to change these policies.

Coming out has its pluses and minuses. It can open up your social life to other GLBTQ teens and allow you to live openly without having to hide who you are. But it can also cause stress in your family and put a strain on your friendships. For most GLBTQ people, coming out is a major milestone and a life-changing experience. It's like taking off a mask and letting people see who you really are. Many people say that when they decided to come out, it was because they were so tired of hiding who they were that they were willing to take the risk of telling others in exchange for the freedom of living openly.

Feeling Pressure to Come Out

All of this emphasis on being out can put a lot of pressure on you, but there is no rush. People can be ready to come out at different times. Some come out at 14, others at 40. Coming out can be a great and affirming experience. But if you're not ready, it can feel like a disaster.

Dr. Sandy Loiterstein, a clinical psychologist who often works with GLBTQ people, emphasizes this point. She explains, "It's important for teens to know that discovering your identity is a process, and everyone does so in her own time. Teens, especially, can have a tough time figuring out who they are because they are sorting through so many issues at once."

You might feel internal pressure to come out. You can also feel pressure from other sources, such as friends or people in the GLBTQ community. Some people might be saying you need to come out, but others might be giving you completely different messages. Maybe your parents or other people say things like, "I don't understand why gay people have to flaunt it. They should keep it to themselves." Regardless of what others tell you, your first responsibility is to yourself.

> **BEEN THERE**
> "The toughest aspect of not being straight is getting over the obsession with what other people are thinking. It is realizing, finally, that who you are is good enough."—Adrian, 20

How's the Weather Out There?
Deciding If You're Ready
(and If It's Safe) to Come Out

Without a doubt, more teens than ever are coming out. Many studies and news articles, including the Human Rights Watch's *Hatred in the Hallways,* are noting the increasingly younger ages when people are coming out. According to a study by Cornell University professor Ritch Savin-Williams, in the 1970s, the average ages when boys disclosed their sexual orientation to family and friends were the mid-20s. In 1998, the average ages had dropped to 16 to 18 years old. According to a 2000 reader survey by GLBTQ youth group OutProud, the average age when respondents first came out to someone was 16.

Several studies, including one published by the Lucile Packard Foundation for Children's Health, have concluded that one reason many teens are coming out earlier is because they are starting to mature sexually at younger ages. It's probably also due to increased access to information and greater visibility of GLBTQ people in daily life. Today, many teens don't have to wait until after high school to receive positive information about GLBTQ people.

Some teens choose to come out, but that doesn't mean you have to. In fact, in some cases, coming out might not be the best decision, at least for now. Tom Sauerman, a leader in the Philadelphia chapter of PFLAG, advises that it might be better for some teens to wait to come out until they can be reasonably certain it won't jeopardize their safety or overall quality of life at home or school.

Questions to Ask Yourself Before Coming Out

Only you can decide when it's the right time to come out. So it's up to you to make sure you're ready. If you're emotionally ready to come out, you'll have a more positive experience than if you're not. Here are some questions to ask yourself to find out if you're up for being out:

Am I sure I'm GLBTQ?

If you're not certain that you're GLBTQ (and remember, it's okay to be questioning), you might want to wait before coming out. Most GLBTQ people come out in part because they feel the need to have others know what they're feeling and experiencing. If you're not sure if you're GLBTQ, think about waiting. Or you can come out as questioning rather than choosing a label right now.

Am I comfortable with myself?

This can be a challenge. After all, at times you may feel like there's nothing comfortable about being a teenager. If you're comfortable and accepting of yourself, the person you're coming out to is more likely to be comfortable and accepting of you.

Why am I coming out?

Come out because you're ready. Come out to affirm yourself. Come out because you *want* to. Don't come out on a whim, or to get a reaction from somebody, or because anyone else says you should.

Can I be patient with other people's reactions?

It's natural to want an immediate positive reaction from the person you're coming out to, but that won't always be the case. Remember how long it might have taken you to adjust to the idea that you're GLBTQ. Be sure you're ready to give others some time to adjust, too.

The World Around You: An Essential Checklist

Even if you're emotionally ready, there are also some external factors that could influence whether it's a good idea to come out:

1. Is it safe for you to come out?

If GLBTQ people are openly harassed or threatened where you live or in your school and little is done to stop it or to protect them, it may not be safe for you to come out just yet. According to a 2001 Massachusetts Youth Risk Behavior Survey, GLBTQ youth are more than twice as likely as their straight peers to be assaulted or involved in at least one physical fight in school and are more than twice as likely to skip school because they feel unsafe. In a 2001 GLSEN nationwide survey of GLBTQ students, 69 percent of the students felt unsafe at their schools because of their sexual orientation.

2. What is your home environment like?

If your parents are aggressive or otherwise abusive, coming out to them could escalate the abuse. If your parents are extremely homophobic, you may also decide to wait to come out until you have other options or have left home. But some teens, who feel safe and comfortable doing so, come out to their parents because their parents can be a source of support and can help teens deal with harassment from others.

> **BEEN THERE**
>
> "Don't get me wrong. I'm proud of who I am, I just have to be proud quietly because I live in a very small (and small-minded) community. Just last year at my school, a boy people called gay was beaten within an inch of his life. I'm a little scared to be too public about it for now."—June, 19

3. Do you have a support system?

Do you have someone to turn to if the reaction to your coming out is bad? You might have a friend who already knows who can support you, or there are also a lot of groups that can help.

Getting Help with Coming Out

Parents, Families and Friends of Lesbians and Gays (PFLAG) is a national organization that offers a wide range of services, from support groups and help lines to literature. PFLAG has over 460 chapters in towns, large and small, all over the country. Talking to the parent of a GLBTQ person or another GLBTQ person can help you decide whether coming out now is right for you. They can also give you advice about how to do it. To find the chapter nearest you, visit *www.pflag.org*, call (202) 467-8180 (this is a toll call outside the Washington, D.C., area), or email info@pflag.org.

If You Don't Have a Choice: Being Outed

Some teens don't get a choice about coming out. A parent might find a note you wrote to someone else where you mentioned being GLBTQ. A classmate might overhear a conversation you had with a friend. It's possible to be faced with a situation where you are outed without your consent.

> **BEEN THERE**
>
> "I was only 13 when I got into a fight with my mom about a letter of mine she'd found. She had the nerve to tell me to stop acting so 'cuddly' with my girlfriends. 'It's not like you're a lesbian are you?' she shouted. Then and there I told her I was bisexual. She stormed from the room. The following day she admitted that it troubled her and that it would take a little while to get used to it, but she wasn't angry or disappointed in me."—Sarah, 18

Figuring out how to handle being outed can be challenging because you have to deal with being out right away with no warning or time to plan. You might suddenly find yourself in an unsafe position. Or your parent or friend could come to you and tell you that they support you no matter what. Chances are the reality will be somewhere between the two extremes.

Now What? Some Tips for Outed Teens

Being outed can feel like a nightmare. But sometimes people don't react as negatively as you'd predicted they would. They might even be supportive.

But any situation when you can't control the outcome can be scary. So what do you do if you're outed?

Do: Take a deep breath.

Being outed can be very unsettling because you weren't given a choice about it and you might feel like you weren't ready to come out. But it happened, so take a moment to regroup and think about how you want to deal with the situation. It's true that you weren't able to control being outed, but you can control how you deal with it from here.

Do: Assess the situation.

This helps determine what your next move should be. Are you safe? How do you feel? How is the other person (or people) reacting? These questions can help you figure out whether you should try to start talking or maybe get some outside help.

Do: Take action.

Based on the other person's reaction and your own level of preparedness, you have several options. If you feel like you can engage in a conversation, do so. By opening the lines of communication, you have the opportunity to be proactive and take the initiative instead of just reacting to a situation that took you by surprise.

Another option is to do nothing. Deciding to wait can be a positive action. If the situation is still too emotionally charged to attempt a positive talk, or if your attempts at talking fail, it's okay to have a cooling off period. This could be a good opportunity for you to get some help and advice from a friend, an adult, or a GLBTQ group.

A third course of action might be more of a necessity than an option. If being outed has made you fear for your safety, either at home or elsewhere, you may need to get help. It's a good idea to approach an adult for help—a trusted family member, counselor, or someone at a national organization, for example. There are many groups listed in the resource section at the back of this book.

Why Come Out?

People come out for a variety of reasons, and many of them are very positive. Coming out is a way to affirm yourself. It shows others that you are happy with the person you are. It can also be a way to reach out to others by sharing something very meaningful and personal with them.

Some people come out to increase the visibility of GLBTQ people. Right now, society as a whole assumes that most people are straight. Many straight people look at others around them and assume that everyone they see is also straight. Coming out and doing things like wearing a triangle pin or putting a rainbow sticker on your car are ways of challenging these assumptions.

> **BEEN THERE**
> "There were 1,900 students at my school when I graduated—1,900 people who can't assume or pretend that gay people don't exist. And if you look at statistics that as many as 10 percent of people are queer, that means that when I came out there were maybe 190 queer kids who got to hear that they are not going to burn in hell, that they are not perverts, and that they can live their lives."—Brian, 19

Who Should I Tell First?

Many people start the coming out process by telling only one or two people, sort of like dipping your big toe into a pool to test the water. Others choose to tell a lot of people at once. Many decide to come out to a friend or sibling first because they believe they will get a better reaction from him or her than they might from a parent.

It's definitely a good idea to choose someone who you think will be supportive. For many, their parents are the last people they want to tell. For others, parents are the people they feel they can go to with anything and are who they want to come out to.

BEEN THERE

"I have come out to my brother. He is younger than me by a year. I felt like I needed to tell someone close to me and he was the one. . . . It has brought us closer."—Elena, 20

There are two big reasons why it's important to take care in selecting the first person you come out to. For starters, if you have a positive first experience, you will feel better about the prospect of coming out to other people. Having someone react positively is a boost to your self-esteem.

Secondly, if the first person you come out to is accepting of you, then you have additional support as you come out to others and someone you can talk to about how you're feeling. This person can also be great to practice on when you're preparing to come out to others. It's very comforting to finally have someone you can be honest with.

Mom? Dad? I Have Something to Tell You: Coming Out to Your Parents

You've given it a lot of thought, and you're ready to come out. So how do you do it, especially to (gulp) your parents? The possible ways to come out are as diverse as the people who decide to come out. There isn't one perfect method for coming out, but some ways are more positive than others.

Be Prepared

Do your research.

Start by testing your parents' reactions to GLBTQ people. Mention a GLBTQ character on a popular TV show. Bring up an issue like GLBTQ civil rights or queer people being allowed to adopt children and see what their reactions are. Keep in mind, these are only hints. Even if a parent thinks GLBTQ people should have equal rights, this doesn't mean they'll be completely calm when they find out it's their own son or daughter they are talking about. And the opposite can also be true.

Knowing their son or daughter is queer might make parents think about being GLBTQ in a different, more positive way.

Gather resources from groups like PFLAG, HRC, and OutProud. These organizations and others have reading lists and brochures for both you and your parents. Even if your parent doesn't read what you give them right away, they may later. And while you might feel awkward about coming out to a parent and then handing them a book, they are more likely to read something you give them than they are to do research on their own.

Be patient.

Coming out to your parents is a milestone in your life, and it's a big deal for them, too. It can be tough when someone you really care about has trouble accepting who you are. Give your parents the benefit of the doubt if they don't embrace your sexual orientation or gender identity at first, and remember that you've had a lot longer to accept yourself as GLBTQ.

Pick a good time.

Coming out to your parents the minute they come home from work is probably a bad idea. Keep in mind that you've been dealing with being GLBTQ for a while, but it might come as a complete surprise to your parents. Pick a time when everyone is relaxed and comfortable.

Hope for the best, but prepare for the worst.

Some parents might respond by kicking you out of the house. It sounds harsh, but it happens. Have an idea of where you can go or who you can call if the scene turns ugly.

Coming Out as Questioning?

You may decide to come out to someone as questioning. If you do, you're still going to have to answer a lot of questions. Telling

continued➞

someone that you are questioning may be confusing for someone who needs a label like gay, lesbian, bisexual, or transgender to help understand the situation. A lot of people prefer to come out after they have a more concrete concept of their sexual or gender identity. Some people feel limited by those words and so they identify as "queer," "gender queer," or in another way entirely.

Practice.

Once you've decided you want to come out, practice, practice, practice. Look at yourself in the mirror or practice on your stuffed animals or on the poster of your favorite sports star. It's like giving a speech at school, only much more personal. If you practice what you're going to say, you'll probably sound a lot calmer and clearer when the time arrives.

Coming Out ✓ Checklist

If you haven't checked off each of these, you might want to rethink your decision to come out.

- ✓ I am ready and I am comfortable with myself.
- ✓ I've asked myself why I want to come out, and I'm sure it's for the right reasons.
- ✓ I'm ready to deal with the outcome.
- ✓ I'm ready to provide information.
- ✓ I have a support system.

Having "The Talk"

No matter how much you prepare, there's no telling what your parents' reactions will be. Nevertheless, there are some very common reactions parents have when their kids come out. It may help you to keep these in mind when you prepare for "The Talk."

Reaction: "How do you know?"

Possible response: "How do you know you're straight? It's just something I feel inside."

Reaction: "It's just a phase."

Possible response: "I understand that you're probably surprised by this. This isn't a phase, and I think in time you'll realize that it's who I am."

Reaction: "Why are you doing this to me?"

Possible response: "This isn't about you. It's about me and my relationship with you. I'm telling you this because it's who I am and I want to be open with you. I want you to have a relationship with *me*, not the person you *think* I am, and that means I have to be honest with you."

Reaction: "It's your choice to be this way."

Possible response: "No one knows exactly why people are queer, but most scientists and health professionals believe part of it could be biology. For me, I don't feel that it's a choice. It's just who I am."

Reaction: "You're just saying that because you think it's cool."

Possible response: "I think it's cool to be honest about who I am, and this is who I am."

Reaction: "But your life is going to be so hard."

Possible response: "Life can be more difficult for GLBTQ people at times, and that's sad. But I'll have to deal with other people's prejudice. What's more difficult to deal with is prejudice in my own family, and that's why I need your support."

Reaction: "But I always thought you'd get married and I'd have grandchildren."

Possible response: "Being GLBTQ doesn't mean I'll never find someone to spend my life with, and it doesn't mean I won't have children. Lots of queer people settle down and have families just like anyone else."

Reaction: "It's just wrong."

Possible response: "Who I am is not wrong. I understand that this is a lot of information to take in, and you probably need some time to think about it. But please know that you can bring it up later and I'll be willing to talk about it."

> **BEEN THERE**
>
> "My father's response was simple. He stood up, gave me a hug, and said 'You remember I said I would always love you, right?' I said, 'Yes.' And he said 'I meant it.'"—Scott, 19

Reaction: "How am I supposed to deal with this?"

Possible response: "I know it's a lot to think about. But please remember that I'm the same person you loved yesterday. I haven't changed, you just know me better now. Trust me when I tell you that a lot of parents have been in your situation. It might help you to talk to some of them. There's a group for parents of GLBTQ people. I'm going to give you the contact information for the local chapter. You don't have to call right now, but I hope you'll at least take the information and know there are people you can talk to who won't judge how you're feeling."

> **BEEN THERE**
>
> "My older sister was awful when I came out to her. There were a lot of unprovoked screaming matches between the two of us for a couple of months. She eventually calmed down and is now totally accepting."—Sonia, 19

Now What? After "The Talk"

Family dynamics can change a lot after someone comes out. Coming out can start arguments or, at the very least, spark a lot of questions. Will you want to bring a boyfriend or girlfriend over? How should your parents handle sleepovers? Should the rules that applied to friends of the opposite sex now switch or also apply to your friends of the same sex?

Coming out may be the end of your hiding something, but it's the beginning of relearning your family dynamics. The keys to dealing with these changes are patience and open lines of communication. All of the questions don't have to be answered all at once. They can be addressed as you go along. Talk about the issues you are facing and try to come up with solutions together.

After the coming out conversation, some parents will act like you never told them. They might be hoping it will go away. They may be going through a stage of denial. Parents often struggle with shock, denial, and guilt when a son or daughter first comes out to them. They might hope that you are only going through a phase or they might feel guilty that there was something they did that somehow caused you to be GLBTQ.

Again, remember that coming out is a process for everyone. Give your parents time, but don't assume they're dealing with it. It's good to check in now and then. Mention that you're there and willing to talk to them if they have any questions or issues they want to discuss. You may feel like now you're the parent and they're the kid, but that's normal. They may need your help coping with this change. Continue to encourage (not demand) that they get in touch with other parents of GLBTQ teens. If they do want to talk with you, try to keep conversations civil and productive. These discussions can get pretty heated, but take a deep breath (or several) and try to relate to what they might be going through.

True Coming Out Stories

The GLBTQ youth group OutProud posts real-life teen coming out stories at their Web site, *www.outproud.org*. Reading other teens' stories can give you pointers and also help you know that you're not alone.

Buddies, Amigos, and Pals:
Coming Out to Your Friends

Like many teens, you may choose to come out to one, some, or even all of your friends before you approach the topic with your parents. According to OutProud's 2000 readers' survey, 76 percent told their best friend first, 21 percent told friends at school, 10 percent told friends outside of school, and 7 percent told their parents first.

It's not surprising that many teens come out to friends first. After all, they're usually the people you share the most with and who you probably feel you'll get the best reaction from.

Just like coming out to parents, coming out to friends can have varied results. Some will be supportive, some confused, some upset, and some will have a combination of these feelings and more. Some might even come out to you!

> **BEEN THERE**
>
> "So far, I have only come out to one friend—my best friend—and that was only after he told me that he was bi. It was funny. We were just sitting there and all of a sudden he says, 'I like guys. But I like girls, too.' Then I said, 'Me, too.' It was that simple, and we talk about it all the time now."—June, 19

Coming out to friends first can be great. If they're supportive, they can be there for you if you come out to your parents. But just like with parents, consider all angles before coming out. If a friend is upset by the news, she might tell other people, which could be bad if you're trying to be selective about who knows.

As with parents, it's a good idea to test the waters by trying to gauge your friend's attitudes toward GLBTQ people. Some friends are more mature or may have had more experience dealing with GLBTQ issues. Maybe they have a GLBTQ relative or even a parent.

If you do decide to come out to a friend, follow the same steps as with your parents. Prepare and be patient. It's important to remember that if your friend doesn't react well, it could be because he's heard negative things about GLBTQ people from his parents or other sources. Talk with him about what he thinks about GLBTQ people and why. Assure him that you're still the same person you've always been and you're still his friend—being GLBTQ doesn't change that.

Coming out can change your friendships. You could become closer than ever. Or your friend could be hurt that you didn't tell him before. He could be concerned that you are attracted to him or he might even worry that if you're GLBTQ, maybe he is, too.

Again, give your friend time to adjust and make it clear that you're ready to talk whenever he is. Some friendships do end because one person comes out, but these are extreme cases. Let your friend know that one of the reasons you told him is that you want to be honest with him about who you are. Tell him, too, that you're going to need his support to deal with people who aren't as accepting. Even if he's upset at first, chances are, as with parents, things will get better. And who knows, he might even surprise you by telling you he'd already figured out that you were GLBTQ on his own!

A Lesson on Coming Out at School

Some teens feel safer or more comfortable coming out to a trusted teacher, school counselor, or administrator. Some come out as a means of reaching out for support or guidance or to get help dealing with harassment that's taking place at school. This might be true for you as well.

Adults who are not your parents can be good advocates and can help you deal with issues you're facing. It's important to remember that teachers and other school officials are people just like everyone else—you can never be absolutely certain how they'll react. But because they aren't your parents, in most cases, your coming out won't trigger some of the more extreme emotions your parents might feel.

Some schools' policies make it difficult for supportive teachers to be vocal about their acceptance of GLBTQ people. But it's not uncommon for teachers who are supportive to let students know, in subtle or more obvious ways, their feelings. (And gradually, teachers are starting to come out at school, too.) If your school has a gay-straight alliance, the group probably has a faculty or staff advisor. If that teacher is approachable, she could be a good person for you to talk with when you need the advice and support of an adult.

> **BEEN THERE**
> "In my last year of junior high, I had this amazing Personal Development and Relationships teacher who I think was a lesbian. She taught us about being homosexual and bisexual. I think it was in that class that I actually discovered the term for what I was."
> —June, 19

School counselors are trained to talk with teens about their problems and many of them can be very helpful. Unfortunately, some of them also might be homophobic. School counselors are sometimes, but not always, bound by confidentiality. This means they can't share what you say to them with anyone else, it has to be kept in confidence. In some cases, there is no confidentiality requirement and some schools even require counselors to report certain things to the administration.

Counselors can be great people to seek advice and support from. If you're worried about talking to a counselor because of confidentiality issues, check your student handbook. The school's policy toward confidentiality should appear there. If you don't have a copy of the handbook, one should be available from the administrative office.

As students and advocacy groups work to make schools safer, more accepting places for GLBTQ teens, teachers and staff are learning what it means to be GLBTQ and are better able to understand and support their GLBTQ students.

4 LIFE AT SCHOOL

I can't even think straight.

One of the most challenging parts of being a GLBTQ teen can be coping with life at school. You've got social hierarchies and cliques, teachers piling on the homework, and administrators watching your every move. Meanwhile, you're going through the normal stages of adolescence, which probably have you feeling anything *but* normal. And on top of all that, you're coming to terms with being GLBTQ.

School Life for GLBTQ Teens: The Big Picture

Recent surveys have revealed that life at school can be pretty uncomfortable and even scary for many GLBTQ teens. A national survey conducted in 2001 by the Gay, Lesbian and Straight Education Network (GLSEN) found that 83 percent of the GLBTQ teens had been called names or threatened; 65 percent had been sexually harassed with sexual comments or inappropriate touching; 42 percent had been physically harassed by being pushed or shoved; 21 percent had been physically assaulted at school by being punched, kicked, or hurt with a weapon; and 31 percent had been harassed because of their gender expression (the way they dressed or acted).

Other surveys in Massachusetts and Vermont have had similar findings: GLBTQ teens are more likely to get involved in fights at school that require them to receive medical attention, more likely to be threatened or injured with a weapon, and (not surprisingly) more likely to skip school because of concerns for their safety than their heterosexual peers.

> **BEEN THERE**
>
> "In ninth grade, my second day at public school, I was walking down the hall and a young male said the word that wounds every gay teenager—fag. From there on things snowballed. Daily, more and more people would use those hate words: fag, homo, queer, sissy. Eventually, things moved from words to also violence and pranks. I even had death threats."—Robert, 15

The picture isn't all bad, though, and it's changing. There are some very exciting things happening in schools all across the country that are improving life for GLBTQ students. Kevin Jennings, Executive Director of GLSEN, states, "From policy makers to parents, an increasing number of people are realizing the urgent need for LGBT students to receive equal treatment in our public schools. And more and more of them are willing to advocate for this cause." GLSEN still says the majority of GLBTQ high school students are regularly harassed by their peers, but as of March 2003, it also had 1,680 student gay-straight alliance clubs (GSAs) in 46 states and Washington, D.C., registered with its Student Organizing Department.

Feeling Invisible . . . or *Too* Visible

Feeling invisible is something that most GLBTQ people experience at one time or another, regardless of their age. It's difficult to grow up and not see many positive representations of people who are like you. It might even make you feel like you're the only one.

Is Anybody Else Out There?

As you walk through the cafeteria, the air is buzzing with girls talking about boys, boys talking about girls. And then there's you, who might be interested in boys, or girls, or both, or neither. In situations like this, it's easy to feel like a square peg in a round hole.

Visibility can be a problem not only in the cafeteria, but also in the curriculum. Debates are taking place all across the country about whether GLBTQ topics should be included in what you learn at school. Unfortunately, in most places they're not. In some districts, teachers can even get into trouble for mentioning queerness to their students. There are other places, however, where teachers are allowed and encouraged to integrate queerness into the curriculum. But if your classes don't include any mention of GLBTQ people, it can seem like you just appeared out of nowhere.

> **BEEN THERE**
> "In high school, the fact that I was aware of my differentness made my experience difficult. However, the ability to come out afforded me the confrontation that didn't allow me to shy away from my reality. By the time I graduated, I had a fairly good idea of what to expect from others and myself."—Adrian, 20

This fact is important: there are a lot of GLBTQ teens out there. Many of them are going through situations and dealing with issues that are very similar to the ones you're facing. It's important that you feel good about yourself whether you're GLBTQ or straight.

Four Ways to Fight Feeling Invisible

Here are some positive steps to keep from feeling isolated:

1. Research your GLBTQ "roots."

The next time you are assigned a project where you can choose your own topic, think about researching some of your GLBTQ roots. Write about poet Walt Whitman, painter Georgia O'Keeffe, composer Peter Tchaikovsky, singer Bessie Smith, or pro tennis player Dr. Renée Richards. Offer a history lesson on the Stonewall uprising and how it shaped the GLBTQ rights movement. Learn about the people who came before you, their failures and their triumphs. It will help you appreciate what a long and rich history queer people have.

2. Get in touch with other GLBTQ teens.

You can meet people through local GLBTQ organizations, online, or through other avenues. It's important to talk to people who understand what you're going through and who can support you. Plus, it's satisfying when you can support someone else in turn.

3. Get involved in creating change.

Join, or even start, a GSA or get involved with a local or national GLBTQ group. It's a great way to meet people, and it feels good to roll up your sleeves and accomplish something positive.

4. Give yourself opportunities to shine.

Take part in activities that give you a chance to feel good about yourself and maybe even show off a little. These don't have to be GLBTQ-related. If you're a great singer, try out for that solo in the spring concert or go out for a role in the musical. Take an art class and paint your heart out. Enter an amazing project in the science fair. Show off your runner's form on the track team. Dust off your guitar and start a band. Give yourself opportunities to succeed and enjoy these everyday victories.

I Wish I Could Just Blend In

Maybe the problem is that you feel too visible. If you're subjected to taunts and harassment nearly every time you change classes, a little invisibility might seem like a good thing to you.

A lot of GLBTQ teens probably share those feelings. Remember those statistics from the GLSEN survey at the beginning of the chapter? You can reach out for help and find ways to make that visibility less scary by getting involved in a GSA or working to change your school's environment.

BEEN THERE

"I think the hardest part for me was the social aspect. All of my friends were very supportive. However, seeing the reactions of many of my classmates was extremely disheartening. Seeing that people found it entirely logical to hate me without knowing me not only hurt, but also, as a result, I lost a lot of faith in people. I soon began to wonder, 'If these misconceptions, misunderstandings, or different beliefs are so abundant and difficult for these people to see through or even consider questioning, then what else could be entirely misunderstood? What may *I* need to take a closer look at? To question?' And that's what sparked me to really search for what I thought, not what I was told to think or what everyone else thought, politically, spiritually, socially, and personally. I have become a much more satisfied, fulfilled, and confident person as a result."—Scott, 19

"Being a lesbian or even being perceived as one had its constraints in high school. I was always pretty guarded. My life was school and softball and work. Then I started to date someone who went to the same school and the lid blew off, but no one was saying anything. That, I think, was the worst thing for me. I was being closely watched and no one would say why. But since then, it seems that half the student population felt a need to come out. Sometimes I think I had something to do with that."—Elena, 20

Exercising Your Rights as a GLBTQ Student

Some schools have policies that protect students from harassment based on sexual orientation or gender identity—school officials have a legal responsibility to protect GLBTQ students from harassment. Your school's harassment policy usually is in your student handbook.

If your school doesn't include sexual orientation and gender identity in its policy on harassment, you still have a right as a human being to be safe at school. And you have options for how to deal with harassment.

Teen Heroes:
Changing the Environment for GLBTQ Students

Sometimes it's difficult to believe that one person can make a big difference, but you can. And what's more, you're *not* alone in the fight against discrimination and harassment. Other teens, just like you, are engaged in similar struggles. And many adults are willing to help. You *can* make a difference by standing up against prejudice and asking others to do the same.

National Day of SILENCE

The National Day of Silence participants use a "visible silence" to protest anti-GLBTQ discrimination and abuse. This "visible silence" usually takes the form of a vow of silence for part or all of the school day. Students involved in the action often hand out "speaking cards" with an explanation of their silence and create opportunities to educate others about the issues facing GLBTQ teens.

Founded in 1996, the Day of Silence Project has become the largest student-led action toward creating safer schools for all, regardless of sexual orientation, gender identity, or gender expression. The project has grown from one event with 150 participants in 1996, to events taking place in over 1,900 middle schools, high schools, colleges, and universities across the country in 2002. For more information on the National Day of Silence, visit *www.dayofsilence.org.*

Take a look at how some of these teens fought harassment in their schools.

Jamie Nabozny

Jamie Nabozny suffered such violent abuse and harassment that he was forced to drop out of his Ashland, Wisconsin, high school. Nabozny brought a lawsuit against the school district, and in 1996, a federal court ruled in his favor, stating that the school had failed to provide him with a safe learning environment. The school agreed to pay nearly $1 million to settle the case. The landmark decision set a precedent for similar cases and forced many schools to examine their own policies.

Pat Doe

Fifteen-year-old transgender student Pat Doe took her school to court over her right to express her gender identity by wearing girl's clothing. According to GLBTQ magazine *The Advocate,* Doe's principal had deemed it "disruptive" for a biologically male student to wear "feminine" clothing. In 2000, a Massachusetts appellate court agreed with Doe and she returned to school able to dress as she was comfortable.

Timothy Dahle

In 2002, 19-year-old Timothy Dahle filed a civil rights lawsuit against the Titusville, Pennsylvania, public school system for failing to stop classmates from verbally and physically harassing him. A federal court settlement awarded the teen $312,000 to settle his claims that school officials failed to protect him. The settlement was the first of its kind in Pennsylvania.

Nikki Youngblood

In 2002, a 17-year-old lesbian named Nikki Youngblood filed a federal suit against her Tampa, Florida, school district charging sex discrimination and a violation of her right to free expression. Her high school omitted her senior picture from the yearbook after she refused to be photographed in the feminine "frilly drape" normally worn by female students in their graduation photos. Nikki had never worn tradition-ally feminine clothes to school and felt the jacket and tie she intended to wear in her photo reflected who she was. She said her omission from the yearbook made it seem like she had never attended the school. "If I can change this [for future students], it would be wonder-ful." (At the time of publication, Nikki's case was still pending.)

Filing a lawsuit isn't always the answer, but it is one option. As a result of these cases and similar ones across the country, some schools are voluntarily changing their policies to protect GLBTQ stu-dents from harassment. Many teens see these rulings as evidence that they should not have to endure harassment.

RESOURCE

Legal Assistance

When it comes to fighting harassment and discrimination, you're not alone. There are organizations you can call on for legal assis-tance. Lambda Legal is a national GLBTQ civil rights group that works with legal issues. Visit their Web site at *www.lambdalegal.org* to find the office nearest you. The American Civil Liberties Union (ACLU) has supported GLBTQ civil rights with legal aid since the 1960s. To find out more about recent cases the ACLU has pursued for GLBTQ stu-dents on harassment, GSAs, and same-sex prom couples, visit their Web site at *www.aclu.org.* GLSEN provides support and resources to GLBTQ students and GSAs. Call GLSEN at (212) 727-0135 (toll call out-side the New York City area), email them at glsen@glsen.org, or visit their Web site at *www.glsen.org.*

The Voice of Authority:
Talking to Teachers and Administrators

Teachers, administrators, and other school officials can be some of your greatest allies or they can be the source of some of your biggest headaches.

For some students, even worse than harassment from other students is dealing with prejudice from school officials. According to Human Rights Watch, an international human rights group, many students find discrimination by teachers even more demoralizing and difficult to deal with than anything their peers say or do.

Some school officials and teachers harass teens by making anti-GLBTQ remarks. Some turn a blind eye to harassment by students or other members of the school community. Others tell GLBTQ students that it's their own fault because they invite harassment by "flaunting" who they are.

However it occurs, harassment and discrimination by school staff is unacceptable. There are actions you can take to address them and to make your school safer.

Confronting Authority

Here are some ways you can confront harassment and discrimination by officials or teachers at your school:

Action: Approach the offending official or teacher.

Calmly and rationally, tell him how his speech or behavior makes you feel. Explain that when he ignores or participates in harassment, it sends a message to other students that it's okay.

Action: Tell a parent, guardian, or other adult.

A parent can be your best ally in standing up to bullies, especially if they're other adults. Confronting an adult can be very intimidating, so it's a good idea to have the support of one or more adults.

Action: Tell an administrator.

If the perpetrator of prejudice is a teacher or other staff member, report her to an administrator such as a principal or vice principal. If the person is an administrator herself, approach the school superintendent or the school board. If you're going that high up in the chain of command, it's especially good to have an adult backup—a parent, a lawyer, someone from a national organization, or a combination of them.

On Your Side: Getting Support from School Staff

Teachers and administrators can also be very sympathetic to the situations of GLBTQ students. Some teachers do speak up when they hear anti-GLBTQ language or see physical harassment.

If you're struggling with discrimination at school, think about talking to one of your more approachable teachers. If your school has a GSA, find out who the advisor is and approach him. He may turn out to be one of your best advocates at school.

As with coming out, it helps to be prepared.

1. Consult with a group such as GLSEN, the ACLU, or Lambda Legal about what your rights are at school.

2. Research how students in other schools have had success in confronting issues with teachers or school administrators.

3. Prepare your case with detailed notes, witnesses, and examples.

4. Be calm and rational. If you're overly emotional, the authorities might try to dismiss you as overreacting.

5. Keep it simple. State your problem as briefly as you can and stick to the facts.

6. Listen. There are two sides to every story. If you keep the lines of communication open, you're more likely to have a positive result.

> **BEEN THERE**
> "I actually found out that my math teacher was a lesbian. After I graduated we ended up becoming friends."—Sarah, 18

Club Life: Gay-Straight Alliances (GSAs) and Other Queer-Friendly Activities

A Gay-Straight Alliance, or GSA, is a student-led school club that aims to create a safe, welcoming, and accepting school environment for all students, regardless of their sexual orientation or gender identity.

GSAs have received a lot of coverage in the media. Some school districts have attempted or are attempting to block their formation. Your right to form a GSA in your school is protected by law. There are two laws specifically that apply—the First Amendment (freedom of speech and assembly) and the federal Equal Access Act (equal treatment of all noninstructional, student-initiated clubs). All over the country, students are fighting back and standing up for their rights to form GSAs.

The OFFICIAL Ruling

U.S. District Court Judge David O. Carter made a landmark decision on GSAs. He stated in his ruling, "To the extent that the [school] board opens up its school facilities to *any* noncurriculum related group, it must open its facilities to *all* student groups." For more information about legal rights and GSAs, visit *www.aclu.org/safeschools*.

BEEN THERE

"I cofounded the GSA at my school. My friend and I wrote the appropriate letters and had the appropriate meetings with the principal, we found a faculty advisor and a place to meet, chose our meeting time and group name, and submitted it all to the principal. It was an uphill battle, during which we came head-to-head with the principal several times, but we managed to do some good things, like hold events for National Coming Out Day and the National Day of Silence. The group was definitely controversial, but we helped to raise a lot of awareness."—Brian, 19

Common Questions and Answers About GSAs

You may have a lot of questions about what Gay-Straight Alliances do. Here are some common questions about GSAs and their answers. All of this information and much more is available from GLSEN. To find out more about GSAs, or even to start your own, visit *www.glsen.org* or visit the GSA Network at *www.gsanetwork.org*.

Q: Who gets involved in GSAs?

A: GSAs welcome any student who feels that harassment and discrimination against GLBTQ people, their families, and their friends is wrong.

Q: How many GSAs are there?

A: GSAs can be found in public, private, and parochial high schools and middle schools of various sizes all over the country. Estimates are that over 1,600 GSAs and GSA-type groups have been formed at schools in the United States over the last 10 years. GLSEN states that nearly 20,000 students are directly involved in GSA activities each year.

Q: Do people in GSAs talk about sex?

A: That's not the purpose of a GSA. GSAs meet like any other club at the school, but the activities range from discussions of gender roles or what it means to be queer to working on projects like creating displays for gay pride month or organizing GLBTQ-awareness activities.

How Do I Start a GSA?

If you are interested in starting a GSA at your school, here are some basic steps that you can take:

1. Find out and follow your school's guidelines.

You establish a GSA the same way you would any other school club. Look in your student handbook for your school's rules for starting a club. There may be guidelines or a process you need to follow, for example, writing a club mission statement.

2. Find a faculty advisor.

Consider teachers or staff members who you think would be supportive or who have shown support for GLBTQ issues. Your school may have guidelines about who is eligible to be a club advisor.

3. Find other interested students.

GSAs are for both GLBTQ and straight students. Straight students who feel that anti-GLBTQ discrimination is wrong are often strong and vocal GSA members. Look for members all over your school, because the more diverse the GSA is, the stronger and more effective it is.

4. Talk to the administration.

Tell them right away what you are doing and try to get their support. If they're supportive, they can help smooth the way for the GSA with students and teachers—and even the community. If they oppose the formation of the group, inform them (calmly and kindly) of your legal rights to start a club.

5. Pick a meeting place.

Select a place in the school that affords some privacy but is also easily accessible. It could be a classroom, counselor's office, or conference room.

6. Advertise.

Let others know about the meeting through posters, announcements, flyers, word-of-mouth, the school's Web site, and other methods. People may tear down or put graffiti on your flyers or posters. Don't get discouraged. Have a reserve stash so you can post more.

7. Plan an agenda.

Think about what you want to do at your first meeting and plan ahead. You can do anything from holding discussions and playing games to having guest speakers and holding workshops. Visit organizations that support GSAs like *www.gsanetwork.org* or *www.glsen.org* for ideas.

8. Hold the meeting.

A good idea for the first meeting is to discuss why the group is needed, plan what its goals are, and brainstorm about projects for the year.

9. Set ground rules.

At the first meeting, work together to create rules to ensure that discussions are safe, confidential, and respectful of everyone's views.

10. Plan for the future.

Set goals for what you want the GSA to accomplish. Be realistic about what you can do over the course of the year, but don't limit yourself. You might be amazed at what you can achieve!

The previous information is adapted from GLSEN's *10 Tips Toward Starting a GSA in a Public School.*

Moving On:
Deciding If You Need to Change Schools

Unfortunately, some queer teens end up having to change schools because the officials at their current school are unwilling to help, or they ignore or even participate in the harassment.

Making the Change

If you've explored all of your options for bringing an end to your harassment—talking with teachers, administrators, school superintendents, the school board, and people from national GLBTQ organizations—and it hasn't worked, or if you believe you're in serious danger, it might be time to change schools. Approach your parent or guardian and talk with him or her about why you feel it's necessary for you to make the change.

Moving to a new school won't necessarily change things. You may still encounter problems similar to the ones you had at your previous school. It's a good idea to have your parent or guardian contact administrators at your new prospective school to find out their stance on

GLBTQ harassment issues. If their attitude is the same as or worse than your current school, it might be wise to look at other options. You could consider getting legal assistance from a national GLBTQ or civil rights organization. (See page 67 for more information.) Homeschooling or studying for the GED at a local community college are other possibilities. A few large school districts (New York, Los Angeles, Dallas) even have schools—public and private—specifically for GLBTQ students.

Don't Drop Out

Whatever you do, don't drop out. GLBTQ teens often have much higher dropout rates than their straight peers—some studies suggest that almost a third of GLBTQ students drop out because of the violence, harassment, or loneliness they face at school. The 1999 Massachusetts Youth Risk Behavior Survey reported a 20 percent dropout rate among GLBTQ students—that's one out of five teens.

An education is incredibly important, and although it might seem like a good solution at the time, dropping out of school will seriously limit your future opportunities. Don't let a group of ignorant people rob you of your future. Whether you change schools, homeschool, get your GED, or opt for early college admission, getting an education is your ticket to getting the life you want and deserve.

BEEN THERE

"I dropped out of high school after six months of constant torture. Being gay, or being perceived to be gay, affected me very negatively, to the point of being suicidal, because of all the daily harassment. [Now I'm being homeschooled.] But I've found that being gay has opened up so many doors for me. My life would be so incredibly different if I weren't gay. Every once in a while I will think about what my life would have been like if I'd been straight, and well, I don't think that I would be as happy as I am right now. I mean, why would I want to be anyone other than who I am?"—Robert, 15

5 GLBTQ FRIENDS

2 COOL 2B STR8

If being GLBTQ is normal and GLBTQ people are not all that different from straight people, why should it matter if you have queer friends?

If you're out and have close, straight friends, that's great. And if your immediate and extended family have been supportive, that's great, too. At the same time, it helps to know someone who can really understand what it's like to be GLBTQ. It's important to have positive role models and to feel like you're part of a peer group.

For many teens, two of their most influential role models are mom and dad. But in most cases, GLBTQ teens can't grow up to be just like mom or dad because odds are mom and dad are straight. A lot of queer teens haven't grown up with role models or peers they can truly identify with, which can make having a peer group even more important. GLBTQ teens who have GLBTQ friends are more likely to feel comfortable with their sexual orientation or gender identity.

> **BEEN THERE**
> "During high school, I got involved with a GLBTQ counseling/social group. I loved it. It really helped me feel more comfortable with myself. All the other kids who went there were from different schools and even different areas. It was nice because it was like forming our own little community. Every week after the 'session,' which we just called 'group,' we'd go out to eat. We had so much fun."—Sonia, 19

Part of the Family:
The Utterly Diverse, Somewhat Cohesive, Always Interesting GLBTQ Community

One of the best things about being GLBTQ is the sense of community you can feel with other queer people. In fact, one of the ways some GLBTQ people identify one another is by using the word "family." As in, "You know Bobby, the guy in our chemistry class? He's family." Some people even have bumper stickers on their cars that read "family."

> **BEEN THERE**
> "It's like being in your own private club. It's like having an inside joke that not everyone understands. But when you do find someone who understands, there is an immediate connection that goes beyond words and finds itself in common experiences."—Adrian, 20

Just like any family though, we don't always get along. So, you can't assume that all GLBTQ people will tolerate or even like each other. Although we're part of a larger group, we're individuals with our own personalities. Being GLBTQ is a major characteristic to have in common, but it might also be the *only* thing you have in common.

5 Things Your GLBTQ Friends Know that Your Straight Friends Don't:

1. What it's like to question your sexual orientation or gender identity.

2. What it's like to deal with the prospect of coming out.

3. What it's like to live in a world where some of your civil rights are uncertain or not recognized at all.

4. What it's like to have to question whether it's safe to hold your boyfriend's or girlfriend's hand in public.

5. The amazing sense of joy you feel when you are able to say that, no matter what anyone else may think or say, you are proud of who you are.

At first you might feel intimidated by the GLBTQ community. You might worry about not being "queer enough" or not following the "GLBTQ rules." You'll soon discover, however, that the GLBTQ community is as diverse as people can be. Whether you're a drama queen, a jock, a butch, a femme, a gender bender, a girlie girl, a manly man, a transman, a club kid, a preppy, an urban hipster, a country boy, an androgyne, a surfer girl, a granola guy, none of the above, or even several of the above, there is room for you just as you are.

BEEN THERE

"Even though I love my straight friends, it was a huge relief to meet other gay teens. It's nice to have people who totally understand what you're talking about, what it's like to come out, and all of that."—Elizabeth, 17

IMRU2? Meeting Other GLBTQ Teens

Throughout history, queer people have come up with some pretty inventive secret ways to identify each other. In the past, one gay man might approach another and ask, "Are you a friend of Dorothy?" If the man answered, "yes," that meant he was also gay. This phrase, which was a reference to Dorothy in *The Wizard of Oz,* is just one example of the many ways GLBTQ people devised to discreetly identify one another. If you ever come across a T-shirt or sticker that reads "Friend of Dorothy," now you're in on the joke.

(((Gaydar)))

Hey, what's that beeping?! Did you know that the word "gaydar" is now in the dictionary? The latest edition of the *Webster's New College Dictionary* defines gaydar as "one gay person's ability to spot another." Gaydar is short for "gay radar." Does gaydar really work? Some people swear by it; others have never heard a beep. You can decide for yourself.

Regardless if you believe in gaydar, here are some tips that will help you find other GLBTQ teens. Don't worry, they're out there (so to speak).

The Top Four Places to Meet Other GLBTQ Teens

1. Queer community centers and organizations.

Many such groups provide social programs like movie nights, while others offer services like counseling or even help with homework. They should be listed in your local telephone directory or you can search the Internet on topics such as "gay community center + [your city and state]." The National Association of Lesbian, Gay, Bisexual, and Transgender Community Centers *(www.lgbtcenters.org)* and the National Youth Advocacy Coalition *(www.nyacyouth.org)* both have search engines at their Web sites to help you find GLBTQ community centers or youth programs in your area.

A Virtual Community Center

If you can't get to a GLBTQ youth center physically, you can get to one virtually if you have Internet access. The Gay Student Center is an online community for GLBTQ young adults. Registration is required, but it is free and you don't have to give your name, just an email address. The Gay Student Center is located at *www.gaystudentcenter.student.com.*

2. GLBTQ bookstores.

Go to a reading or just show up and casually flip through some periodicals. You could bump into other young people. If there's no GLBTQ bookstore in your area, there could be a GLBTQ section in your local bookstore.

3. Coffee houses or other places where teens and students like to hang out.

This may work especially well if your town has a "gay neighborhood." This can be a great way to work yourself into your community's GLBTQ scene without having to put yourself out there too much.

4. Underage clubs.

They're often fun and going there increases your chances of meeting people around your own age.

A Note About the Bar Scene

If you're underage, hangouts for people over 21 could spell trouble for you because you risk finding yourself in situations you're not prepared for like underage drinking, drug use, and smoking, even though you're just looking for friendship. If you do decide that's where you want to try to meet people, take some safety precautions:

continued——▶

- Bring a friend (or friends) so you can check out the scene and keep an eye on each other.

- If you go by yourself, tell a friend what you're doing and where you're going.

- Think ahead of time about the situations you might find yourself in (not having a ride home, dealing with someone drunk, being offered drugs) and the best way to respond.

- Decide in advance that you're not going to engage in any behavior (drinking, drugs, etc.) that could land you in trouble.

BEEN THERE
"I began drinking at about age 14. For a long time, I thought the community was in the clubs. I figured that was where all the gay people hung out. And I thought that was what I was supposed to do."—Lee, 26

How Do You Know If They're GLBTQ?

If you meet someone in a non-GLBTQ-centered place, it can be difficult to identify whether someone is queer. Even if your gaydar is beeping like crazy, try not to make any assumptions. Subtlety is usually the best tactic when trying to figure out if someone is GLBTQ. Regardless of how out you are, others might not take kindly to you waltzing up to them and asking, "You're queer, right?"

Here are some subtle strategies for figuring out if the person who caught your eye was actually winking, or just trying to get rid of a loose eyelash:

Strategy

Start a conversation and reference something you saw on *Will & Grace* or another show with gay characters in starring roles. If he also watches the show, ask who his favorite character is. Maybe he'll get the hint and drop his own.

Strategy

If you don't mind outing yourself, casually mention something about an ex-boyfriend or ex-girlfriend. For example, if you're in a coffee shop: "Hi, I noticed you sitting here by yourself. I was supposed to meet my [ex-girlfriend/ex-boyfriend] here, but [she/he] couldn't make it. Mind if I sit down?"

Strategy

If you're at a bookstore, bring over a copy of a GLBTQ-themed book. Tell the person you're thinking about buying it and ask if they happen to know anything about it. It doesn't win the subtle award, but it will probably help get the information you're looking for.

Strategy

If you're the plain straightforward type, go ahead and ask. But there's no need to shout, "Hey, are you queer or what?" At least start a conversation first and then slip it in. Think of how you might feel if someone walked up to you demanding to know your sexual orientation or gender identity. Keep in mind that if the person is straight, depending on her attitude, she might be offended by your question, so be prepared for a variety of responses.

Dial In or Log Off? GLBTQ Online Communities

The Internet is a great place to meet and talk with others. Whether you're an experienced surfer or you've barely gotten your feet wet, finding others on the information superhighway is surprisingly easy.

Some Places to Start on the Web

Here are some sites that offer a variety of resources:

- *www.outproud.org* is sponsored by OutProud, an organization for GLBTQ youth. The Web site has a huge amount of information and a wide variety of resources, including a forum to

continued➞

talk with other teens, a resource library, true teen coming out stories, and a special page for transgender teens.

- *www.youthresource.com* is sponsored by Advocates for Youth. It offers peer counselors, lots of information on topics from coming out to activism, and a number of other resources.

- *www.gaystudentcenter.student.com* is on online community of GLBTQ high school and college students. The Web site contains discussion boards, articles, and links to helpful resources.

- *www.youth-guard.org* provides support services on the Internet for GLBTQ youth. Sign up for one of three email lists to receive information and support from caring adults and young people.

- *www.glsen.org* is for more activism-minded students, but it's still a great place to get in touch with other teens. They can put you in touch with local chapters and GSAs as well as other gay student groups.

Many Web sites sponsor scheduled chats, guest speakers, chat rooms, bulletin boards, and some even let you have your own email account. You can chat online with other GLBTQ teens, post questions or conversation topics, talk to peer counselors or adult counselors, and so on.

BEEN THERE
"I've come out to people online, in large groups in chat rooms, which is much easier than in person or one-on-one."—Renée, 19

It might take some trial and error to find what you're looking for. You might end up visiting several sites before you settle on one, or a few, that you want to explore further.

The Internet: Stay Safe as You Surf

Here are some things to think about and a few key questions to ask in order to help you stay safe as you surf:

Who sponsors the site?

Could they have an ulterior motive that could influence the content? (For example, something to sell you.)

Who's giving that advice?

Keep in mind that on some sites, and especially bulletin boards, you don't know who is answering or how valid the information is. You probably want to save serious questions for sites with a counselor or other expert responding.

What kind of information do they want from you?

Some sites require you to register before using them. Be wary of sites that require you to give information beyond a user name and a password. **And *never* give out your address or your home phone number.**

Who are you talking to?

You can never be absolutely sure who you're talking to online, so be careful and make decisions about what you say accordingly. Don't give out personal information like your phone number or where you live. Meeting alone with someone you became acquainted with online could be very dangerous. Your new friend could be exactly who he says he is—or he might not be. It's best to wait until you can be accompanied by a parent, guardian, or other trusted adult.

Be *very* wary of anyone who requests a photo immediately and *never* send a revealing photo over the Internet. It's just not safe, and it's definitely not smart. You never know where that picture will show up.

Ditch anyone who uses inappropriate or suggestive language—you don't need to waste your time on people who make you uncomfortable or don't speak to you respectfully.

To find out more about being safe and having fun online, take a look at OutProud's online brochure titled "Watching Out for Yourself in Online Relationships: Tips for the Lesbigay Teen." To access it, visit OutProud's Web site at *www.outproud.org.*

Queer Compadres: GLBTQ Friendships

Be yourself. As you're looking for GLBTQ friends, keep in mind that not just any GLBTQ person will do. As with all friendships, you need to be true to yourself. It's great to be friends with other GLBTQ people, as long as they're people you would pick to be your friends otherwise.

Don't waste your time on people who try to talk you into doing negative things, like using drugs and alcohol, just because they're GLBTQ. Queer people are just like everyone else—everyone is different. You'll like some and you won't like others. But don't lower your standards just to make friends. Knowing who you are and sticking to your beliefs ensures you won't become involved in unhealthy relationships or activities.

Thinking about all of this may have you feeling like it's the first day of school all over again. Try not to worry, you'll make some good friends. Just to prove it, here are five reasons why:

1. You are true to your beliefs.

2. You are proud of who you are, or at least you're working on it.

3. You respect others' opinions.

4. You have a lot to offer.

5. You know that life can be very serious, but there's still a lot of room for fun.

BEEN THERE

"My senior year I realized I was living for myself and no one else. I had no one to please but me. I hung out with the people I wanted to and didn't worry about people other than that. I did the things I wanted to do and spoke my mind whether or not someone else agreed with it."—Sarah, 18

Straight But Not Narrow: Other Friends

Straight friendships are no less valuable than GLBTQ ones. In fact, it's good to be friends with a wide variety of people. Exposure to different viewpoints helps make you a more well-rounded, considerate person.

"That's sooooo gay! Um, no offense."

It can be easy to lose patience with your straight friends if they make remarks that you feel are insensitive or ignorant. But try to be patient with them. Bring it to their attention and calmly explain why they hurt your feelings or upset you. Many times you'll find that it's just a misunderstanding and your friend didn't realize how what she said sounded, or she thoughtlessly said something out of habit, or she didn't think it would be offensive. We all have things we can learn from each other. Give her a chance. You might be the first GLBTQ person she knows.

However, if you have a friend who is repeatedly offensive or even abusive and who doesn't care whether you're offended, you might want to rethink the friendship. GLBTQ or straight, do you really want to be friends with someone who treats you or anyone else like that?

Bridging the Gap

After you come out to a straight friend, he might feel uncomfortable. Maybe he's still getting used to it, but maybe he just isn't exactly sure what your coming out to him means. Does it mean you're going to start dressing, acting, or talking a different way? Will you still want to be friends or will you want new GLBTQ ones instead? Does it mean you want to date him?

These questions might come up right away, down the road, or not at all. But take time to address them if they do come up, because it will make your friendship stronger. Also, knowledge is contagious. The next time your friend hears someone demeaning GLBTQ people, he might just intervene. And that's how people and society start to change.

6 DATING AND RELATIONSHIPS

I'm not a lesbian, but my girlfriend is.

In 2001, Long Island Gay and Lesbian Youth (LIGALY) held a GLBTQ prom. The theme was "Free to Be" and over 200 teens from as far away as Brooklyn and Queens showed up and partied down. The prom received a lot of media coverage, including from the *New York Times*, which dubbed the event "America's First Suburban Gay Prom."

The dating scene for GLBTQ teens might seem a little grim, but options do exist. Maybe your town doesn't hold a GLBTQ prom, but queer teens can find ways to get together and have fun. As you become more comfortable with your sexuality, you may find yourself dating a little, or maybe even a lot. The important thing to remember: whether you're an experienced dater, just beginning, or just thinking about it, you decide how to run your love life.

Soul Searching:
Figuring Out If You're Ready to Date

When you're a teen, there can be a lot of pressure to date. But the fact is, not everyone is ready. If you're still trying to figure out who you are, it can be difficult to try to start a relationship with someone else.

> **BEEN THERE**
> "To be honest, I haven't really dated anyone. I've only ever kissed one girl, and I don't even speak to her now. I have found a few people through GLBTQ Web sites and such, but mostly people to talk to, and a few have become my friends."—June, 19

Trying to Fit In

Dating can be a lot of fun, but it can also feel like torture if you don't feel free to date the people who you're really interested in. Many queer people end up in straight relationships or dating situations either because it's expected of them or as an attempt to fit in, or to try to change their feelings of being queer.

It's common for GLBTQ teens to try to change or fit in. Some teens date people of the opposite sex in an attempt to hide their sexual orientation or in the hopes that it will make them heterosexual. Some even engage in heterosexual sex to try to deny their true identities.

If you find yourself in these situations, ask yourself if you're dating contrary to your wants and needs because you feel like you have to. For some, these dates can be good, safe experiences. For others, they can be miserable. If it's making you unhappy, you don't have to go on these dates. If, on the other hand, these dates are more about friends hanging out, then it's okay. The key is to be true to yourself and honest with the person you're spending time with.

Dating to Figure Things Out

If you're questioning, dating might be a positive way for you to explore your sexual orientation. You can meet new people, have some fun, and figure some things out. Dating can help you answer some questions, but sex won't. Engaging in sexual activity for the purpose of figuring out who you are is a bad idea, and it's not necessary. Being GLBTQ is about a lot more than who you sleep with, so you don't need to have sex to become certain of your sexual orientation.

The No-Holds-Barred Bare Naked Truth

YOU DON'T HAVE TO HAVE SEX TO FIGURE OUT YOUR SEXUALITY. PERIOD. EXCLAMATION POINT.

And you don't even have to date. If you're really feeling conflicted about your identity, the thought of dating might not appeal to you right now. The important thing is to listen to yourself. Don't do anything you're not ready for, because if you push yourself, things will just become more stressful. Remember, everything will sort itself out if you give it (and yourself) a chance.

Am I Ready? A Dating Checklist

This checklist can help you figure out if you're ready. So, before you check out the dating scene, be sure to check off each of these items:

1. I am confident in myself.

2. I don't feel like I need someone else's approval and I don't feel the need to please others to the detriment of myself.

3. I am confident I can say "no" if someone pressures me to do something I don't want to do.

4. I can be respectful of others' feelings and beliefs and won't try to force them to do something they're not comfortable with.

5. If things don't work out with one person, I know there are plenty of others out there.

Who Gets the Check? GLBTQ Dating Basics

Most of us get our ideas about romance from movies and TV, and there aren't many examples of Troy sweeping Dave off his feet and living happily ever after, or of Janet and Becky waltzing off into the sunset. The absence of any GLBTQ dating role models can make some teens nervous about the idea of dating.

GLBTQ Dating Q&A

It's natural to have a lot of questions and some confusion as you enter the queer dating scene. Most likely, a lot of what you've learned is probably modeled after boy-girl dating. So what happens if it's boy-boy or girl-girl? Here are some common questions and answers:

Q: What's a GLBTQ relationship supposed to be like? How do I know what to do if we're both boys/girls?

A: What's any relationship supposed to be like? Starting to date is a confusing time for everyone, but it probably feels a lot more confusing if you're GLBTQ. A lot of our behavior is based on ideas about female and male roles in relationships. Being GLBTQ is a great opportunity to throw those stereotypes out the window and just be yourself. Let your personalities dictate what the relationship is like. As long as you're true to yourself and the relationship is healthy, you're off to a good start.

> **BEEN THERE**
> "I would love to just approach someone and start talking to them if I think they're attractive, but it's hard for me because I've never had the chance to date women before. As soon as I came out, my former girlfriend scooped me up, so I really don't have any other experience. I turn into a shy 14-year-old and forget how to talk."—Sonia, 19

Q: How do I figure out who should pay?

A: More and more people are going Dutch—each person pays for his or her share. Many teens don't have a lot of pocket money to start with, so it helps if you split the tab. If only one person is going to pay, it's usually the person who initiated the date.

Q: Where is a good place to go on a date?

A: The standards are dinner, a movie, or someplace like a coffee shop or arcade where you can hang out. Nothing wrong with those—they're classics. GLBTQ-friendly places like social events at queer community centers and underage clubs are great because you can be yourself.

Q: Is it true that GLBTQ people are more promiscuous?

A: Myth alert! That's not true. And you certainly shouldn't feel like you have to engage in sexual activity to find out if you're GLBTQ, to prove something to someone (even yourself), to make another person happy, or for any other reason. Just like anyone else, you should take the time you need to be sure you're absolutely, positively ready.

Q: If I don't know a lot of GLBTQ people, will I just have to settle for dating whoever is around?

A: Absolutely not. One of the down sides about being GLBTQ in high school is that you probably have fewer dating options than some of your friends. Nevertheless, you don't have to settle. If someone doesn't interest you, you don't have to date him or her just because he or she is GLBTQ.

What's My Type?

Among the most common misconceptions about GLBTQ people is that we pair off according to type—butch with femme. First of all, words like butch (people having a traditionally masculine gender expression) and femme (people having a traditionally feminine gender expression) don't even begin to take into account the full spectrum of GLBTQ people. Second, attraction just is, whether you're GLBTQ or straight. You can be attracted to anyone.

The concept of butch and femme have been around a long time. In the past, they were often used as a visible means of declaring an interest in the same sex. The roles of butch and femme continue to influence some GLBTQ relationships.

They also color the perception many straight people have about GLBTQ relationships. Many of the ideas are based on the concept that there has to be a "male" and a "female" in every relationship, and regardless of the sex or gender of those involved, each must take one of these roles. The truth is, people have been operating with these traditions for so long that they started to think of these "traditions" as laws of nature. But they're not.

Some people do prefer this kind of dynamic in their relationships, and that's their choice. But you also have a choice—you can be in a relationship with anyone regardless of what labels you take for yourself, even if you don't take any labels at all.

BEEN THERE

"The dynamics of queer relationships is an issue that I don't think is addressed very often. The ideas of butch and femme within relationships, as well as the idea of *not* having those concepts in a relationship, are things that are stereotyped about the queer community, but rarely addressed in a plain way. At least in my experience of being bisexual, it can be really confusing to feel like there are specific male/female roles in a different-sex relationship and then to not have that framework, or familiarity, in same-sex relationships."—Gwen, 18

The GLBTQ Dating Scene: A Word of Caution

Meeting other queer teens can be difficult. But it might not be as hard as you think. If you decide that it's time to date, be sure that you're safe in how and where you meet people. Some young people, distressed about being GLBTQ or just desperate to meet someone else who is, hook up with the first person who pays them some attention.

Just like in any dating situation, sometimes people don't have your best interests at heart. Although it's the exception rather than the rule, sometimes older or more experienced GLBTQ people take advantage of younger or less experienced ones, offering them sympathy and compassion while luring them into sexual situations. It can be very comforting to have someone listen and pay attention to you, and maybe he's the first GLBTQ person who's shown an interest in you, but take time to think about whether that person is thinking about you or only about his own interests.

Being "Out" on a Date

It's great to hold hands with your sweetie or give her a little kiss while you're walking down the street. Unfortunately, public displays of affection (PDA) aren't something queer people can, in many cases, take for granted. It's important to be aware of where you are and who else is around.

It's one thing for your hand-holding to cause grandma's jaw to drop in surprise, it's another for it to attract the attention of some people who might want to hurt you. If PDA could be a safety issue, then you may want to give it a second thought. It's a lot better if the date is memorable because it went so well than because someone got hurt.

Showing a LITTLE Affection

It can be nice to show a little affection, but it's just bad manners to explore the inside of your partner's throat with your tongue in public. Queer or straight, no one wants to see that.

Assessing the Situation

Homophobes aren't lurking in every shadow, but they are out there and some of them are dangerous. Unless you're on extremely familiar or otherwise safe turf like a GLBTQ establishment, before leaning in for a quick peck, do a quick check of your surroundings.

- Are there a lot of people close by?

- What's the feeling you get from them by looking at them? What are your instincts telling you?

- Are people minding their own business or are they a little too interested in yours?

- Are you in a place that's open or easily accessible, or are you in a confined space where it would be tough to leave quickly?

Keep in mind that the degree to which you're open about your identity will always be up to you. Be realistic about your safety. Hopefully, before too long, society will discover other things to worry about and a little queer PDA won't cause a second glance.

Knowing Looks and Open Stares

Even if you're not displaying affection, people might know by looking at you two that you're on a date. It might draw some attention. For example, maybe the woman at the table next to you nearly dropped her fork when you reached over and touched your date's hand. Assuming you're in a safe situation, it's up to you to decide whether you're comfortable with that.

Maybe you couldn't care less and say, "Let them stare until their eyes dry out." But if you're uncomfortable, this might be one of those times to remind yourself that there is absolutely, positively nothing wrong with being GLBTQ. It's natural to feel self-conscious when you start dating. In fact, queer or straight, lots of people feel self-conscious on first dates. Don't worry—it will get better. The longer you are out, the more comfortable with yourself you'll be.

And don't assume people are looking because they're upset. Maybe they think you look like a cute couple, or perhaps the woman who almost dropped her fork wishes her daughter could find such a nice girl. You never know.

Singing the Breakup Blues

Sadly, not all love stories end happily. All romantic relationships can run into problems, and GLBTQ ones are no different. Dealing with a breakup can be rough. Sometimes it can be tougher for GLBTQ teens because you might have limited options for other people to date or people to talk with about the breakup.

If you're going through a breakup, you can do things to help take care of yourself. Here are some tips that may help you get over the breakup:

1. Don't act like it didn't happen.

Breakups hurt—that's why the word starts with "break." It's okay to be upset.

2. Let it out.

Write a "Top Ten Reasons I Am Upset" list in your journal. Turn your radio on and sing along at the top of your lungs to the most depressing songs you can find. Go for a run and tackle the toughest hill in the neighborhood.

3. Talk a good friend's ear off.

Sharing your thoughts with another person can help you decompress. Don't forget your friends online. If you don't have someone local you can talk to, an email pal might be the next best thing.

4. Take care of yourself.

Try to eat well, exercise, and get enough sleep. Your depression will only get worse if you lie in bed all day, curled up in your bunny slippers eating potato chips.

5. Take it one day at a time.

You won't be over a breakup in a day, or even two. But time does help and you will start to feel better. You might even be ready to stop sticking pins into that little doll you named after your ex.

In addition to the usual breakup complications, GLBTQ teens sometimes have another issue to face—some people who know about the breakup may be pretty insensitive. Unfortunately, some people don't think GLBTQ relationships are as meaningful and valid as straight relationships. When you go through a breakup, they don't understand why you're so upset.

These people might say uninformed things, like encourage you to give being straight "another chance." Dealing with issues like that can be annoying and painful when you're busy trying to mend a broken heart.

Here are some possible responses to some insensitive comments:

Clueless Remark	Possible Response
"It didn't work because you're not queer in the first place."	"It didn't work because we weren't right for each other. I'm having a tough time dealing with this and I could use your support."
"Will you go back to dating girls now?"	"If you and dad split up, would you start dating women?"
"It's not like it was a real relationship anyway."	"It hurts when you belittle how I feel. Whether you approved of the relationship isn't the issue. This isn't about you, it's about me."

Abusive Relationships:
Recognizing Them and Getting Help

Recent studies about teen dating violence and abuse show that GLBTQ teens are just as likely as their straight peers to find themselves in abusive relationships. Estimates range from 10 to 30 percent of teens experience an abusive dating relationship at some point. A lot less is said about partner abuse in GLBTQ relationships, but it definitely happens. Studies also suggest that dating violence in GLBTQ teen couples, like with opposite-sex couples, is probably underreported.

Dating and relationship violence for GLBTQ teens is very similar to abuse and violence in straight teen relationships. But GLBTQ teens may also have to deal with homophobia and ignorance about GLBTQ relationships in addition to the abuse from their partner. Abusive partners also can threaten to out the person being abused.

GLBTQ teens can struggle with ideas of what relationships should be like because of a lack of positive queer role models. This can make abuse harder to recognize because you don't expect it or because you've never seen it addressed in GLBTQ relationships. No matter who you're dating, you have the right to be treated with respect by your partner. There is no excuse for abusive behavior of any sort, period.

Here are some *facts* about dating violence and relationship abuse for GLBTQ teens:

- You never deserve to be abused. No one does.

- The abuse is not your fault. It is the fault of the abuser, no matter how much that person may blame you. ("You shouldn't have said that, you know I have a temper.")

- Abuse can take many different forms. It can be physical, emotional, sexual, psychological, verbal, or even social.

- Abuse usually happens in cycles. There may be a lot of "kissing and making up" afterwards, but then the abuse starts all over again.

- Abusers often try to isolate their partners from family, friends, and teammates. The person being abused often feels scared and alone.

- Abuse is about control and power, *not* love.

Here are some *myths* about dating violence and relationship abuse for GLBTQ teens:

- Abuse and violence don't happen in GLBTQ relationships. They're straight problems.

- If there's violence in a GLBTQ relationship, then it must be mutual or a "fair fight."

- There aren't any resources for GLBTQ teens in abusive relationships.

The truth is, abuse can happen in any kind of romantic relationship and it doesn't matter what the sexes of the partners involved are. There's nothing fair or mutual about an abusive relationship—it's about one person controlling and hurting another. There *are* resources for GLBTQ teens in abusive relationships. People and organizations are becoming more aware of the dating violence in GLBTQ relationships. See page 98 for ways to get help.

Emotional Abuse

Emotional abuse can be harder to recognize than other forms of abuse, because it is often less obvious than physical abuse. Emotional abuse can include name-calling, insults, your partner putting you and your interests down all the time, jealousy and possessiveness, and attempts to control who you see, what you do, what you wear, and what you eat.

A partner may tell you that you're fat or stupid or that nobody else would ever want you. Maybe she is extremely jealous and always demands to know where you are and who you're with. Or maybe she controls you with her temper or with the fear of what she does when she loses her temper (like breaking things, humiliating you in public, or hurting you). Perhaps she makes extreme demands on your time (even when you have important school or family commitments) and flirts, pouts, and eventually loses her temper if she doesn't get it. Maybe she tells you in subtle or obvious ways that you could never find or you don't deserve anyone better than her. Whatever the method, it's still abuse. Emotional abuse can take a lot of different forms, but they all have the same result—they make you feel bad about yourself.

> **BEEN THERE**
> "The healthiest relationships are based on mutual respect. They are partnerships that give you energy and bring intimacy into life without harming your other relationships."—Jeremy, 20

Abusive Relationships: Getting Help

It can be very difficult to break out of an abusive relationship, but there are people who are willing to help. The National Domestic Violence Hotline is a free resource, call 1-800-799-SAFE. The National Organization for Victim Assistance has a database of resources for victims of different kinds of crime, including relationship abuse. Call 1-800-TRY-NOVA. RAINN (Rape, Abuse and Incest National Network) is a free resource for those who have experienced sexual assault or abuse. Call them at 1-800-656-HOPE. Look in your local or state phone directory for additional resources including: domestic violence coalitions, rape or sexual violence crisis centers, and GLBTQ resource centers.

Physical Abuse

Physical abuse is often the first thing that comes to mind when people think about abusive relationships. Physical abuse can include hitting, slapping, shoving, grabbing, kicking, hair-pulling, biting, pinching, and throwing things. Physical abuse is often accompanied by threats of violence or an ongoing fear that violence will erupt.

Sexual Abuse

Physical abuse can also be sexual in nature. Sexual abuse can include being forced or coerced into doing sexual activities you don't want to do or aren't ready for. The abusive partner may use emotional blackmail like "If you really love me . . ." to pressure you into sexual activity. It's important to remember that even if you have a sexual relationship with your partner, you always have the right to say no to sex of any kind. It doesn't matter how long you've been dating, it's your body. Even if you've been sexual with your partner before, you still have the right to say no now. If your partner doesn't respect that and tries to force you emotionally or physically, he's being abusive.

The Abusive Relationship Self-Test

An abusive relationship can be hard to recognize when you're in it. Here are some questions to help you take a closer look at your relationship. If you answer "yes" to any of these questions, you could be in an abusive relationship:

- Does your partner call you names, insult you, or make you feel badly about yourself?

- Does your partner often demand to know where you have been (or are going) and who you talked to?

- Does your partner humiliate you in public or in front of friends or classmates?

- Does your partner make all of the decisions in the relationship or get ugly when you disagree with his or her decisions?

- Do you ever avoid activities you enjoy or hanging out with your friends because you feel like it's not worth dealing with your partner's temper later or you're scared of what he or she will do?

- Does your partner try to control what you wear, what you eat, and how you spend your time?

- Are you ever afraid of your partner?

- Does your partner ever blame you for her or his behavior, telling you that it's your fault she or he hit you, scared you, or lost her or his temper?

- Do you find yourself making excuses to others for your partner's behavior, especially how he or she treats you?

- Does your partner try to keep you from spending time with family or friends?

- Is your partner inconsiderate of your feelings? Does she or he tell you that you are blowing things out of proportion or that you are overreacting when you try to discuss her or his behavior?

- Is your partner jealous of your time and want to be with you constantly?

■ Does your partner ever coerce you or force you into engaging in intimate physical behavior, such as sex?

■ Has your partner ever physically assaulted you, regardless of whether he or she caused a bruise or other injury?

■ Has your partner ever verbally assaulted or threatened you?

■ Has your partner ever destroyed any of your possessions?

■ Has your partner ever threatened to kill himself or herself if you left the relationship?

If one or more of these sounds familiar, you may be in an abusive relationship.

Stopping Abuse

Abuse is never acceptable. If you want it to stop, you can either leave the relationship or try to change things. If you are in an abusive relationship and you decide to have a talk with your partner, here are some tips that could help:

1. Tell him how his words and actions make you feel.

2. If he is apologetic and seems genuinely remorseful, it's up to you whether you want to give him another chance.

But be very careful. Abusive relationships often have cycles. The abusive person is very apologetic for what he's done and swears he will "never do it again." Things are good for a while, but then the old pattern of abuse can start again.

3. If the abuse starts again, it's time to get out.

Everyone makes mistakes, but chances are the abuse is part of a cycle, and it's only a matter of time before that behavior shows itself again.

If you decide to get out of the relationship entirely, you have some different options. You can call national hotlines (see page 98) or crisis hotlines, like the Trevor line, for help. You can look for local resource options in a phone directory or by searching on the Web. Domestic violence organizations, rape crisis centers, and GLBTQ resource centers are all good places to start.

It can be difficult to reach out to people you know, but trusted adults can be a good resource. Your parents, older siblings, the sponsor of your school's GSA, or a trusted school counselor are all possibilities. If you're not out to anyone, it can be more complicated and you may prefer, at least at first, talking to someone at a local or national organization.

You Deserve R-E-S-P-E-C-T

Soul singer Aretha Franklin had it right. Respect is the word to remember in relationships. Keep these tips in mind to be sure your relationships are healthy.

React to your partner's negative behavior by talking to her or getting out of the relationship.

Express your ideas and thoughts. If your partner tries to make you think or act a certain way, he's bad news.

Spend your time with people who are supportive and positive. This includes your partner.

Pledge to yourself that you value your own well-being too much to tolerate an abusive relationship.

Expect to have a partner who respects you and who you respect in turn.

Choose for yourself. Don't let your partner dictate your decisions about who you talk to, what you eat, how you dress, or anything else.

Talk to someone if you are in an abusive relationship. Tell them you need help putting a stop to the abuse. It's okay to ask for help.

7 SEX AND SEXUALITY

Love is a many gendered thing.

If you're thinking about relationships and dating, you may also be thinking about your sexuality and what sex, at some point, might mean for you. Like relationships, sexuality can be a confusing and complicated issue. What works for one person, may not for another, so it can help to think about what *you* have questions about and feel comfortable with.

Especially for GLBTQ teens, information can be pretty difficult to come by. You may feel that what you're hearing about sex from your friends, family, school, or religious leaders doesn't apply to you. If most everyone around you is assuming you're straight, sorting through those assumptions to get the information you need about sex, much less making decisions about sex, can start to seem impossible.

Making good decisions for yourself about sex is tremendously important. When are you ready and why? What boundaries do you want to set for yourself physically? How well do you need to know or how much do you need to care for someone before you're ready? What are you comfortable doing? What do you think sex is and what does it mean to you? Do you know how to stay safe sexually (and can you talk to a partner about it)? Are you able to talk to someone you're dating about what your limits are for keeping yourself healthy physically and emotionally?

That's a lot to think about, and trying to process all of those considerations can feel overwhelming. But don't feel discouraged. Information is your best friend. What you know about yourself, about what you believe, and about sex and sexuality is what will guide you through your questions and help you make decisions.

Beliefs—what you think is right and wrong, what you think is important—are what people use to figure out what their boundaries are and to make decisions. People often get their beliefs from their family, culture, and religion. You may be comfortable with these beliefs or you may be exploring different beliefs that make more sense to you. If you can be open with your family, a spiritual leader, or others around you, they may be able to help you think through your questions and help you get more information. If you come from a value tradition that strongly disapproves of queer people, figuring out what you believe in is even more complicated. It can help to talk about your feelings with a counselor who works with GLBTQ people or with someone from PFLAG.

The other information you need is the technical stuff about sex, sexuality, and how your body works. Questions like "What is queer sex?" and "What is safer sex?" are important ones to answer. This chapter is designed to help you recognize the myths or misinformation you may have come across about queer sex and sexuality and to give you facts.

When information about sexuality is presented at school or at home, the usual assumption is that your partner will eventually be someone of the opposite sex. Many parents don't think to raise the issue of GLBTQ sexuality when they're talking about sex. They may focus their concerns on anatomy, pregnancy, abstinence, or sexually transmitted infections (STIs). Also, if your parents are straight, their understanding of GLBTQ physical relationships is likely to be limited or nonexistent.

When schools teach topics about human sexuality, they often avoid discussing GLBTQ relationships. A 2001 report by the Sexuality Information and Education Council of the United States (SIECUS) showed that only 13 states included gender identity and sexual orientation information in their schools' teaching plans.

All of this might leave you feeling invisible or at best only partially informed. For example, advice like "wait until you're married" isn't particularly useful for GLBTQ people who, at least for now, can't be legally married.

There's a lot for you to think about before you decide what is right for you. This chapter will help give you the tools you need to make the choices that are healthiest for you right now.

Making Sound Decisions About S-E-X

Becoming aware of your sexuality is a major part of adolescence whether you're queer or straight. It can involve a lot of thinking about sex and what it means for you. It also involves making a lot of decisions.

Deciding to be sexually active is a big choice and a major milestone for many reasons. It can involve new physical experiences, intense emotions, and responsibilities. Depending on the situation, you might find yourself needing to know a lot of things at once—from understanding how to keep yourself safe and healthy to being able to communicate honestly with a partner. So taking the time now to determine boundaries and get accurate information is a great way to respect yourself, whatever decisions you make.

You may decide not to have sex, to experiment with some activities but not others, or to actually have sex.

In some ways you might feel ready, in other ways you might not. You may have a lot of curiosity and a mix of facts and misinformation buzzing around in your mind. And that can lead to a lot of questions and ideas.

Q: I have sexual urges. Does that mean I'm ready?

A: As you become more sexually aware, you're also changing emotionally. You may be having physical urges, but you may also feel confused, worried, anxious, or unsure about acting on those urges.

There isn't a magic age when someone's ready to have sex. The factors that contribute to being emotionally and physically ready are unique to each individual.

Q: Can I be sort of ready?

A: If you feel like you're ready for sexual intimacy, that doesn't necessarily mean that you *are* ready for sex. And it doesn't have to be all or nothing. From holding hands and hugging to making out and beyond, there are lots of activities that can express affection and be both physically and emotionally pleasurable. You could be ready for some, but not necessarily all of them. If you're doing something that makes you feel uncomfortable, listen to that feeling. It may be an indicator that you're moving beyond what you're ready for.

You need to decide where you want to set your boundaries. Learning how to set those boundaries is part of the process of maturing into someone who's comfortable being affectionate or sexual with someone else. And part of setting boundaries is being able to communicate with your partner even when the topic is embarrassing or difficult. So think about what you want and what's important to you.

Talk with your partner about your feelings, and ask what your partner feels ready for, too.

Gradually exploring is usually safer and more comfortable than jumping right in. And it also allows you to move at your own pace and decide one step at a time what you're ready for and what, for now, is too much.

Q: Isn't everyone else having sex?

A: It's true that there are many teens who engage in sexual activity. There are also many teens who choose not to or who set boundaries about their sexual activities. Doing it and feeling like you made the right decision can be two different things. Consider some research results:

- SIECUS surveyed American adults about the first time they had sex and found that more than 80 percent of them were teens when they first had sex. However, many of those people, when looking back, aren't happy with their decisions. SIECUS reported that 65 percent of women and 45 percent of men regretted their decisions and thought they'd had sex at too early an age.

- Recent studies show that rates of teen sexual activity have been steadily decreasing. The Centers for Disease Control (CDC) and the Henry J. Kaiser Family Foundation reported in 1999 that half of all ninth- through twelfth- grade students had had sex. This was down from 54 percent in 1990. They also report that the number of teens who've had multiple partners has declined as well. While no one knows exactly why, these trends have been consistent over the past several years.

Statistics show that half of your peers are doing it; but they also show that half aren't. There will always be people who try to tell you that "everyone" is doing it, but that simply is not true. If you decide you're not ready or you're not interested, you'll have a lot of company.

Researchers have also found that some teens who say they've had sex are stretching the truth. With all of the pressure to have sex, it's understandable that some teens feel the need to lie about their experiences. Some tell stories to get attention, to feel more mature, or to get people to quit asking if they're having sex. Knowing that they could be lying gives you another reason not to base your decision on what your friends might or might not be doing.

If your friends really are having sex, you may feel left out or like they're growing up and you're not. Keep reminding yourself that what might be right for them isn't necessarily right for you. Only you can decide what you're ready for. Besides, if they're really good friends, they won't pressure you to do anything that's not right for you.

When the Pressure's ON

It can be hard to say no to sex when someone is pressuring you. You may have to let them know that you want the pressure to stop. Here are some possible responses:

Pressure	Response
"You should really try it. It's great."	"I'm sure it *will* be great . . . when I'm ready."
"Don't be such a prude. Everyone is doing it."	"Not really. Lots of people might say they're doing it, but not all of them are telling the truth. If you really care about me, you won't put pressure on me."
"Sex is no big deal."	"If that were true, we wouldn't be talking about this. And if sex is no big deal, why are you putting so much pressure on me to have it?"
"Maybe you're just not mature enough to have sex."	"I'm mature enough to make responsible decisions about things that are important to me and that will affect my life. I'm mature enough to stick to my decisions. And I'm also mature enough not to pressure my friends into doing something they've decided not to do."

Q: Sex is only right when you're in love, right?

A: For some, sex is an expression of love between two people. For others, it is a physical pleasure that does not have to be accompanied by love. Even so, most people agree that the most fulfilling sexual experiences are those that happen with someone you care about. Still, being in love doesn't mean you have to have sex.

> **BEEN THERE**
>
> "Don't let the sex be the reason you are with the person you're with. Being sexually active is nothing compared with the emotional and mental connection that is important in the relationship."—Elena, 20

Q: But I'm in a relationship . . .

A: Love and sex are not synonymous. You can love someone, yet not feel ready to have sex. It doesn't mean you don't care about this person. It means you don't want to move to that level of physical intimacy just yet.

One of the absolute best things about being in a relationship is the firsts. The first time your eyes meet and you smile at each other, the first time you hold hands, the first time you kiss, and if everything feels right, the first time you have sex. But the thing that makes those firsts so special and memorable is that they happen only once, and they're most enjoyable when you're both ready.

Q: What if I don't want to keep having sex?

A: Maybe you've already started having sex. If you're having sex and are not feeling good about it, remember that you can stop. Just because you've had it doesn't mean you have to keep having it.

Have an open discussion with your partner. If he really cares about you, he'll understand and will be supportive. Bringing it up may feel a little scary or embarrassing, but having sex with someone who you don't feel like you can talk to about it could be a signal that you've gotten into something too soon or with the wrong person.

Ways to say NO
to a boyfriend or girlfriend

Saying no to a partner who wants to be sexual can be extremely difficult. But you don't owe it to anyone to have sex with them. You owe it to yourself to make the decision that is best for you.

Here are some tips for responding to pressure from a boyfriend or girlfriend:

Pressure	Response
"If you love me, you'll have sex with me."	"Sex and love are two different things. If *you* love *me,* you'll let me choose when I'm ready. Besides, if you push me into making a decision I'm not comfortable with, it could ruin our relationship. Is having sex worth that risk to you?"
"You say you love me, so prove it."	"I prove to you that I love you every day by respecting your thoughts and decisions. Why don't you prove you love me by doing the same?"
"It's not like you can get pregnant."	"Maybe not, but having sex means a lot to me. If I decide to have sex with you, then I'm deciding to share something very personal and intimate. Acting like sex is nothing to you tells me that you don't respect how important the decision is for me. I'm not comfortable with that."

continued——▶

"It's not like you're going to get married. So what're you saving yourself for?"	"I'm saving myself for when I'm ready and when I've found the right person. If you can't respect my decisions, you're not that person."
"C'mon. I know you're not a virgin."	"Just because I've had sex before, doesn't mean I want to have it now. And it doesn't mean that I'll do it with just anyone. I respect myself, and I give serious thought to who I'm intimate with."
"But we've had sex before."	"Yeah, and I wasn't ready. So now I'm going to wait until I am. If you can't support my decision, you're sending me a message that sex means more to you than my feelings and our relationship."

What Do You Think?

You may have a lot on your mind right now about your sexuality and having sex. Maybe the questions and situations you've been reading about have been familiar or maybe you're asking yourself other questions. Perhaps you're just starting to think about these issues or perhaps you're already becoming sexually active. Either way, the more you know about yourself, the healthier your decisions, emotionally and physically, will be about your boundaries, activities, and partners.

Here are some questions it may help to ask yourself and think about while you're deciding if you're ready to be sexually active:

- Am I comfortable with myself and my body?

- Do I respect myself and have a strong sense of my own self-worth?

- Am I comfortable talking about sex and about my boundaries with my partner?

- Do I feel comfortable saying no when I need to?

- Have I thought about what being sexual could mean for me emotionally and what it could mean for my relationship?

- Do I understand that I don't need to have sex to be loved? Do I know that just because I love someone, I don't need to have sex to prove it?

- Do I know what STIs are and how they're transmitted? Do I know about safer sex? Am I able to talk to my partner about safer sex? Am I confident enough to insist on using protection for any sexual activity?

- Do I know that I can change my mind at any time about having sex? Do I understand that I can say no at any point, even at the last minute, even if I've told someone I will have sex, even if I've said yes before?

- Do I know that if I have sex, I don't have to keep having it?

- Do I feel clear about my beliefs and values about having sex?

Five Myths (and Truths) About GLBTQ Sex

Arm yourself with the facts before you decide to have sex. Sex and sexuality can make you nervous and confused, especially when you're GLBTQ, because there is so much misinformation about queer sex. Don't let your decisions about sex be influenced by myths and stereotypes.

Maybe these are some of the myths you've heard about GLBTQ sexuality:

Myth #1: Having sex is the best way to help me figure out if I'm GLBTQ.

Lots of people are faced with questions like "How do I know for sure?" when they're coming out. Some people might even tell you that if you've never had sex with a person of the same sex, you can't be certain of your sexual orientation. Many people grow up believing that being GLBTQ is about who you have sex with.

Truth #1: It's not. It's about who you are as a person and it's part of your personal identity. Having sex won't prove or disprove anything that you didn't already know or suspect. So being sexually active won't help you figure anything out. And it could have negative results if you're not ready to deal with the emotions it can stir up or aren't comfortable insisting on safer sex.

> **BEEN THERE**
> "Don't straight people know they're heterosexual before they've had sex?"—Renée, 19

Myth #2: GLBTQ people are promiscuous.

Some people have the idea that being GLBTQ is only about sex, and therefore having sex is the primary focus of GLBTQ people.

Truth #2: The fact is, GLBTQ people aren't any more promiscuous by nature or in practice than straight people. Being GLBTQ doesn't mean you have to engage in sexual activity. Having sex is a personal decision, regardless of whether you're GLBTQ or straight.

Myth #3: Oral sex isn't really sex.

Some people consider it to be a very intimate activity, while others attach less importance to it. Some people feel it's an activity you do as part of getting ready to have sex, while others consider it to be sex. For them, it's one of their primary sexual activities. How you feel about it is something only you can decide.

Truth #3: Here are some truths to consider about oral sex. There's no denying that oral sex is significant sexual contact. You definitely can get or give many sexually transmitted infections (STIs) through oral sex. Oral sex involves very intimate physical contact, and you're making a choice to share something very personal with someone else.

It's important to communicate clearly about this issue with your partner. If oral sex is a big deal for you, but your partner doesn't feel the same, it can cause a problem. You could end up feeling like your partner doesn't appreciate the value of physical intimacy and how important sharing that is to you. Determining whether you're ready to engage in sexual activity includes making important decisions about oral sex.

Myth #4: Gay men only engage in anal sex and lesbians only engage in oral sex.

This goes down in the queer hall of fame as one of the biggest, most pervasive sexual myths about GLBTQ people. This myth comes from people who don't know or understand what it means to be queer, so their ideas about queer sexuality are limited and sometimes downright strange.

Truth #4: There is a whole range of sexual activities that GLBTQ people engage in. Some gay men rarely or never have anal sex and some lesbians rarely or never have oral sex. It's up to each individual to decide what he or she likes and is comfortable with.

BEEN THERE

"Sex is not the end-all, be-all. Having sex does not make or break one's identity. Enjoy what you do because you want to be doing it, not because you think it's what you should be doing."—Adrian, 20

Myth #5: GLBTQ people are the only ones who have to worry about getting HIV/AIDS.

In the early 1980s, when the HIV and AIDS epidemic was first starting in the United States, gay men were severely impacted. People grew to associate gay men and queer people in general with AIDS, even though all different kinds of people were becoming sick.

Truth #5: *Everyone* has to worry about HIV/AIDS, GLBTQ or straight. Contrary to what some people believe, gay men have not cornered the market on HIV/AIDS infection. In fact, according to the United Nations' AIDS joint program (UNAIDS) in their 2002 report, 42 million people are living with HIV or AIDS worldwide. Over 19 million are women. Two million of the 5 million people who became infected in 2002 are women.

It's not who you are, but what you do that puts you at risk for getting HIV/AIDS. And you can get HIV/AIDS from only one exposure. It's not the number of times you have sex but rather the kind of sex you have that puts you at risk. If you make healthy choices and practice safer sex (more on this later), you can minimize your risk of HIV exposure, but there is no such thing as totally safe sex for anyone—GLBTQ or straight.

Educating Others

Advocates for Youth has a program that helps teens become peer educators. They encourage teens to get involved in activities that help educate their peers about sex, including sound decision-making and HIV/AIDS and STI prevention. For more information, visit their Web site at *www.advocatesforyouth.org*.

The Big Picture: STIs & Pregnancy

Some other issues to consider are sexually transmitted infections (STIs) and pregnancy. Yes, pregnancy. Being queer may make it less likely, but it doesn't make it impossible. (For more about this, see page 118.) And if you're thinking about or are already engaging in sexual activity, you definitely need to worry about STIs whether you're GLBTQ or straight. STIs are infections that are passed from one person to another primarily through vaginal, oral, or anal intercourse, although intimate contact without intercourse can also transmit certain STIs. STIs are serious business. Unfortunately, one unprotected encounter can result in some serious and long-term consequences.

Just the Facts About STIs

1. STIs are common among teens.

According to the CDC, one in four of all new STI infections each year occurs in teens. Out of the roughly 15 million new cases a year, almost four million are teens.

> **BEEN THERE**
> "I have always addressed safer sex because those things are so essential. It's important to know where to go for condoms and testing."—Elena, 20

Need More Information
About Sex, STIs, and Being Safe?

Here are some resources that are full of useful information about anatomy, sex and sexuality, and STIs. While they are not GLBTQ specific, they are all helpful for (and sometimes written by) teens and are GLBTQ respectful.

Books:

Changing Bodies, Changing Lives: A Book for Teens on Sex and Relationships by Ruth Bell and the Teen Book Project (New York: Three Rivers Press, 1998). For ages 14–19, this book contains thorough and nonjudgmental information on sexuality and a wide range of emotional and physical issues affecting teens, including: general emotional and physical health care, sexual harassment and violence, STIs, pregnancy, eating disorders, and positive role-modeling.

The "Go Ask Alice" Book of Answers: A Guide to Good Physical, Sexual, and Emotional Health by Columbia University's Health Education Program (New York: Henry Holt and Company, Inc., 1998). In a Q-and-A format, this book provides straightforward, nonjudgmental, and detailed answers to often difficult questions about physical, sexual, and emotional health. It also has a thorough resource list.

Web sites:

Coalition for Positive Sexuality
www.positive.org
This is an excellent sex information site for teens. Down-to-earth in tone and thorough, it answers many questions about sex and offers information (in English and Spanish) about safer sex and contraception. It also offers a discussion board where teens can learn with and consult each other about sexuality issues.

Go Ask Alice
www.goaskalice.columbia.edu
In a Q-and-A format, Columbia University's Go Ask Alice provides factual, in-depth, straightforward, and nonjudgmental information about sexuality, sexual health issues, and relationships.

continued——▶

Iwannaknow
www.iwannaknow.org
The purpose of this site is to provide a safe, educational, and fun place for teens to learn about STIs and sexual health. Sponsored by the American Social Health Association (ASHA), it also contains a parent's guide.

It's Your (Sex) Life
www.itsyoursexlife.com
The site's goal is to provide reliable and objective information about sexual health issues to young adults. It focuses on communication, HIV and STIs, pregnancy, and contraception. Sponsored by the Kaiser Family Foundation.

SEX, ETC.
www.sexetc.org
This site is by teens for teens and a place where teens can get accurate, up-front information about their sexuality, as well as a place to get their questions answered. Topics addressed include STIs, sexual orientation, masturbation, sex education in schools, virginity, and dating violence. Operated by the Network for Family Life Education and Rutgers University.

Hotlines:

CDC National Information Hotline: 1-800-232-4636
The Centers for Disease Control's (CDC) Information Hotline is the world's largest health information service. It operates 24 hours a day, seven days a week. Trained information specialists answer questions about HIV infection and AIDS, STIs, and more. Specialists provide referrals to appropriate services including clinics, hospitals, local hotlines, counseling and testing sites, legal services, health departments, support groups, educational organizations, and service agencies throughout the United States.

continued——▶

American Social Health Association's (ASHA) STI Resource Center Hotline: 1-919-361-8400

The ASHA Hotline provides anonymous, confidential information on STIs and how to prevent them. It also provides referrals to clinical and other services. Operates Monday through Friday from 9AM to 6PM EST.

2. HIV/AIDS still has no cure.

There are many other STIs besides HIV/AIDS, but HIV infection among teens is a serious issue. The Kaiser Family Foundation reports that teens and young adults from the ages of 15 to 24 account for 42 percent of the new HIV infections worldwide. It's true that many people with HIV/AIDS are enjoying a much better quality of life than ever before, but anyone with HIV/AIDS will tell you that living with HIV/AIDS is *not* easy. Researchers have made significant advances in developing better medicines for HIV/AIDS, but there still is no cure. Some people believe a cure will come soon, so they think they don't have to be so careful. It's easy to give in to the moment, and it's hard to imagine that you could really become infected. But it's a very risky gamble. You could be betting your life even if you think they'll soon find a cure.

3. Women who have sex with women transmit STIs, too.

Women being sexual with other women can spread sexually transmitted infections. According to a 1999 article in the journal *Archives of Internal Medicine,* a study of nearly seven thousand women who identified as lesbians showed:

- just over 17 percent reported that they have or have had an STI
- only 21 percent had ever suggested to a partner that they practice safer sex

In another survey of women who sleep with women published in 2000 in the *Journal of the Gay and Lesbian Medical Association,* 26 percent reported they had a history of sexually transmitted infections.

RESOURCE

GLBTQ-Friendly Medical Professionals

If you don't feel like you can talk to your doctor and can't find a local clinic, the Gay and Lesbian Medical Association (GLMA) has a link at its Web site that will allow you to search for a queer-friendly doctor near you. The address is *www.glma.org* or you can call them at (415) 255-4547.

Pregnancy

Some teens, terrified by the idea they might be GLBTQ, have sexual relationships with people of the opposite sex to prove to themselves and others that they are "normal." Others engage in heterosexual sex to find a community that they think of as being more "normal" than the queer community.

Make no mistake about it, regardless of your age or your sexual orientation or gender identity, if you're an anatomical female who has vaginal intercourse with an anatomical male, you can get pregnant. And even if you're gay or trans, if you are an anatomical male, you can get a female pregnant.

Safe vs. Safer Sex

What's the difference? There is no such thing as totally safe sex. However, if you choose to be sexually active, practicing saf-*er* sex can significantly help reduce the chances of infection or pregnancy.

Here are some basic facts you need to know about safer sex:

Fact: Bodily fluids such as semen, vaginal fluids, and blood are the primary means through which sexually transmitted infections are passed from one person to another.

It's not always necessary to exchange bodily fluids to become infected, but they are a primary means of infection for many STIs and the only means through which HIV can be transmitted.

Fact: You need to use *latex* barriers to protect against infection.

Whether it's in the form of condoms, dental dams, or gloves, latex is your best friend when it comes to safer sex. Latex is relatively cheap and you can buy latex barriers at most drug stores, convenience stores, or even mega stores. Some rest rooms are even equipped with condom dispensers. Also, many public health clinics, including Planned Parenthood and HIV/AIDS organizations, give out free condoms. Some also give out dental dams.

A few other useful things to know about latex:

- Latex condoms are the best choice for safer sex. Some "natural" condoms are made from lambskin. Infections like HIV can still pass through lambskin, but latex stops them. (If you're allergic to latex, see page 120 for information on polyurethane barriers.)

- Dental dams are square pieces of latex designed to cover the vulva, vagina, or anus during oral sex. Dental dams protect the mouth from exposure to bodily fluids that could contain bacteria or viruses.

- Dental dams can be harder to find than condoms. One alternative is to make a dental dam out of a condom by unrolling it, cutting off the closed end, and cutting it along a long end. But this only works with an unlubricated condom and also one that is not treated with a spermicide. And yes, plastic wrap can be used as a substitute for a dental dam, but it must be the kind that isn't perforated at all—plastic wrap with the little holes in it is useless.

Fact: Latex is essential not only for vaginal or anal sex, but also for oral sex and mutual masturbation.

Infections can be passed through activities like touching your partner with your hand or fingers if you have cuts or scratches on your hands or fingers. You may not always see small abrasions, so it's best to use a latex glove. They're pretty easy to find—most drug stores have them either in the First Aid section or with insulin test kits, which are often by the pharmacy counter.

Price check on condoms!

Nervous about going into the drug store to buy protection? Keep in mind that it's better to see the pharmacist to ask where the gloves or condoms are than to see her when you have to fill a prescription because you caught an STI. If you're really nervous, consider asking a friend to go with you.

Fact: You need to be kind to latex. Latex only works as long as it's undamaged.

Heat and oil-based lubricants can damage latex. Don't keep latex barriers like condoms in a wallet or somewhere else where they'll be exposed to prolonged heat. Also, don't use condoms or other latex barriers with oily substances like baby oil, petroleum jelly, solid shortening, cooking oils like olive oil and vegetable oil, animal fats like butter, massage oils, or peanut butter. Oils and petroleum-based products destroy latex.

The best bet for a lubricant is one that's water-based like K-Y Jelly or K-Y liquid, for example, which you can find in most drug or even grocery stores. Some GLBTQ book stores sell lubricants. Silicone-based ones will work as well. Most lubricants will say on the container or packaging whether they are oil-, silicone-, or water-based.

Fact: Polyurethane barriers have also been certified by the FDA to prevent the transmission of HIV.

Polyurethane condoms, gloves, and dental dams *do* protect against HIV infection and the transmission of other STIs. The condoms can also be used to prevent pregnancy. However, polyurethane barriers are more expensive, harder to find, and according to the FDA and *Consumer Reports* the condoms are more prone to breaking. They are usually recommended for people who are sensitive to latex or have a latex allergy.

Fact: Anal sex is a high-risk behavior and needs extra protection.

It is one of the highest risk behaviors for transmitting an STI, whether between partners of the same *or* the opposite sex. The inside of the rectum is a very porous mucous membrane that can transmit an infection, including HIV contained in blood or semen, directly into the bloodstream.

Barriers to Safer Sex: Lack of Communication

Talk with your partner about safer sex, while the clothes are still on. Talking about issues that may make you shy or nervous is much easier when you're not in the heat of the moment. And talking and thinking about safer sex ahead of time means you're giving yourself the opportunity to be prepared when the time comes. Make a point of knowing where you both stand so that you can respect each others' health and comfort levels. The keys to safer sex are openness and respect.

> **BEEN THERE**
> "I had never been intimate with anyone before I was with my most recent girlfriend. But before we started to get sexually active, I had her show me her recent test results for STIs."—Sonia, 19

Think about how you want to keep yourself safe. It's not always easy to talk about safer sex, but you will need to talk to your partner about it. Even if you're not yet ready for sex, talk with your partner now, so when you are ready, you'll practice safer sex.

Common Arguments Against Safer Sex and How You Can Handle Them

Here are some common arguments against safer sex and the other side of the argument:

continued➡

Argument	The Other Side
"I'm allergic to latex."	It is true that some people are allergic to latex. However, due to wonderful scientific advances, condoms, dental dams, and gloves are now available in polyurethane, as well. A latex allergy is no excuse for not practicing safer sex. (For more about this, see page 120.)
"Safer is too complicated."	If safer sex seems like a pain, how complicated is getting an infection or getting pregnant because you didn't feel like or didn't take the time to use protection?
"It doesn't feel as good with a condom, dental dam, or glove."	What doesn't feel good is when you and your partner don't take into consideration each others' health and well-being. Show you care about yourself and your partner by practicing safer sex.
"It's embarrassing to talk to a partner about using protection."	Talking about safer sex can be scary and hard. But look at it this way— if you're going to be sexual with someone, you should at least feel comfortable and respectful enough to get past a little embarrassment. Take a deep breath and insist that you both use protection.
"My partner says he's clean, and I trust him."	It's great that you trust your partner, but that doesn't make you safe. Your partner may truly believe that he is free of infection, just as you might believe the same about yourself, but lots of STIs don't have obvious symptoms, so it's important to be tested, then tested again a few months later. Out of concern and respect for yourself and your partner, play it safer.

continued ⟶

"My partner and I are both virgins, so we don't need protection."	Even if you're both virgins, practices like anal sex can be risky because of the chance of infection due to possible exposure to bacteria. Also, if you're engaging in heterosexual sex, you can get pregnant even if it's your first time. Make sure your sexual experiences are healthy, both emotionally and physically.
"Talking about safer sex spoils the mood."	Talking about safer sex shows your partner that you care about both of you. (And nothing spoils the mood like dealing with an STI.)

Barriers to Safer Sex: Drinking and Drugs

One of the biggest barriers to keeping yourself safe is drinking or doing drugs. Even with the best intentions, you can find yourself in the middle of activities or situations you would have avoided if you'd been sober.

Need proof? According to a 2003 report from Columbia University's Center on Addiction and Substance Abuse:

- teens who are 14 and younger who drink are twice as likely to have sex as those in the same age group who don't drink

- teens who are 14 and younger who use drugs are four times as likely to have sex as those who don't use drugs

- teens 15 and older who drink are seven times as likely to have sex as those who don't drink

- teens 15 and older who use drugs are five times as likely to have sex as teens who don't use drugs

If your judgment is impaired, chances are greater that you'll have unsafe sex.

Drugs + Sex = Risky Behavior. The only good decision is one that you make when you're 100 percent sober.

8 STAYING HEALTHY

Queer by nature, absolutely fabulous by choice.

Let's face it, adolescence when you're a queer or questioning teen can be an amazing, thought-provoking time. It can also be seriously stressful. When you're focused on issues like figuring out if you're GLBTQ, choosing whether to come out, and deciding how you feel about relationships and sex, it's easy to let your health take a back seat. But your physical and mental well-being is important and needs just as much attention as other aspects of your life.

Researchers from the American Psychological Association (APA) have noted that GLBTQ teens run a greater risk of taking part in potentially unhealthy or dangerous behaviors because of difficulty navigating the teen years. But it was also noted that GLBTQ teens often have sophisticated coping skills and tended to use a broader range of coping resources than their heterosexual peers. GLBTQ teens may also be more likely to develop greater interpersonal problem-solving skills.

These latter findings are good news, because as a GLBTQ teen, you may face different, often more difficult issues than your straight peers. It's even more important that you pay extra attention to your health, so you can have the emotional and physical resources to deal with whatever life throws at you.

Chilling Out: Dealing with Stress as a GLBTQ Teen

Anger, frustration, sadness—it's natural for anyone to experience these feelings sometimes. With all you've got going on in your life, it's normal to be stressed. But GLBTQ teens run an even greater risk of suffering from stress and depression. You'll never be able to get rid of all the stress in your life, but there are ways to make dealing with it a little easier.

> **BEEN THERE**
> "When I'm feeling down I sing or write. I try to do something creative; anything that will get my mind off of whatever is going on at that particular moment."—Robert, 15

Five Great Ways to Beat the Blues

While it's okay to feel frustrated or unhappy with the way things are, you'll feel better if you find ways to deal with those emotions. There are a lot of wonderful things that you don't want to miss out on because you're depressed or stressed.

> **BEEN THERE**
> "When I'm stressed, I immerse myself in literature, trying to find reflections of myself in the outside world."—Adrian, 20

There are a number of great ways to deal with stress on an everyday basis. Invent your own or take a look at these suggestions:

1. Let It Out!

Find a way to express your feelings by talking, writing, dancing, acting, singing, rapping, or drawing. There's a whole range of great ways you can express yourself from the private (write in a journal—for more on this see pages 127–128) to the public (act in a school play). And the more ways that you explore, the better you'll feel and the greater the chance you'll find a talent you never knew you had.

2. Exercise!

Again, it's all about finding something to do that you enjoy. If team sports are your thing, try out for a team at school. If that isn't an option, there may be intramural teams in the community you could join, or try playing pick-up games of basketball (or your favorite sport) with your friends. Classes in dance, yoga, or martial arts may all be options as well. If you prefer to go solo, there are still many things to choose from—biking, skateboarding, skating, running, hiking, lifting weights, dancing, swimming. Any kind of exercise can make you feel better emotionally as well as physically. So get those endorphins pumping and do something great for your body.

3. Eat Well!

There really is a reason why everyone talks up a balanced diet—it keeps your body healthy and happy. It doesn't mean that you can't eat your favorite treats, but the key is everything in moderation. You can have those French fries once in a while, just don't make them a staple of your diet. Good food gives your body the fuel it needs to be strong and resilient.

4. Take Healthy Risks!

Jump into life. One of the best things about being alive is trying new things. Sometimes those new things are scary, like playing on open mike night or asking someone out on a date. Sometimes they're fun, like joining a sports team, traveling somewhere you've never been, or discovering you have a green thumb. When you try new things, you'll have fun and learn a lot about yourself in the process.

5. Get Involved!

It's a lot harder to feel isolated when you get involved and you see that you're not alone. Get involved in the GLBTQ community, whether it's by reading about other GLBTQ people or by meeting some. (See chapter 5 for more on how to do that.) It'll make you feel better to know that there are a whole lot of us around from all walks of life. Volunteering for your favorite cause or getting politically active are also great ways to meet people—both queer and straight—who share your interests.

> **BEEN THERE**
>
> "When I'm stressed, I call my GLBTQ friends or go online and read about other people in my position. Knowing that I'm not alone in how I feel makes me feel better. Also, I keep a journal, and writing always makes me feel better, no matter what's bothering me."—June, 19

Jumping into Journaling

Keeping a journal is a great way to think about your life, work through feelings, and blow off steam. There are many different ways to keep a journal and they can include writing "letters" to people, sketching, and writing poetry, as well as talking about your day or your feelings. (It's probably best to safeguard your journal somehow to maintain your privacy, so that you can feel free to really express yourself.)

You may already be a pro at journaling or maybe you're just getting started. Here's a tactic you can try that may help you let it all out and feel better about yourself at the same time.

1. In your journal (whether it's a notebook or on your computer), write down exactly what is making you stressed. Tell the person who made that nasty comment just what you think of it. Tell that senator that you can't believe he sponsored that anti-queer bill. Whatever you are feeling, let it out.

2. Count the number of negative statements you made, like "I can't believe he . . . " or "I am so sick of . . . "

3. Take a clean sheet of paper or move to a new page in your computer document and make a numbered list. If you wrote three negative things, number the list from one to three, and so on. For each negative sentiment you wrote, write something positive about yourself. It doesn't have to have anything to do with you being GLBTQ or even what's upsetting you. It can be a good way to put things in perspective and get some emotional balance. Here's an example of what this kind of journal entry might look like:

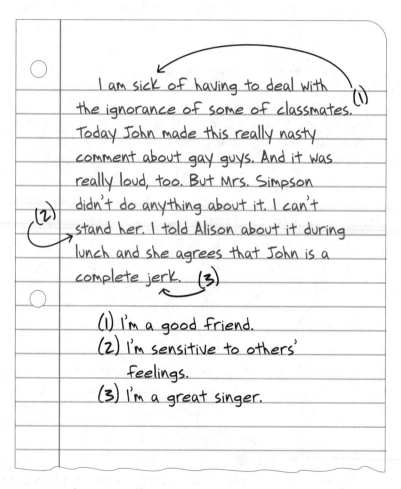

I am sick of having to deal with the ignorance of some of classmates. (1) Today John made this really nasty comment about gay guys. And it was really loud, too. But Mrs. Simpson didn't do anything about it. I can't (2) stand her. I told Alison about it during lunch and she agrees that John is a complete jerk. (3)

(1) I'm a good friend.
(2) I'm sensitive to others' feelings.
(3) I'm a great singer.

No matter how you choose to write in your journal and unwind, just remember three key words: LET IT OUT!

When Stress Turns into Depression

Depression can be a major issue for teens, especially queer teens. There's nothing about being GLBTQ that means you're destined to a life of sadness. But take the usual stresses of being a teen and combine them with confronting homophobia and transphobia in other people and even in yourself, and you have a mixture that can take a toll on your self-esteem. Even when you're not tangling with obvious homophobia and transphobia, it can be really hard to feel like you don't fit in to the world around you. This is true even if you generally feel pretty good about yourself.

Untreated depression for GLBTQ teens can have lethal consequences. Studies, including the Massachusetts Youth Risk Behavior Survey, consistently show that GLBTQ teens are up to four times more likely to attempt suicide than their straight peers. One study in the medical journal *Pediatrics* suggested that queer teens may account for 30 percent of adolescent suicides annually, which can be a pretty scary statistic to think about.

> **BEEN THERE**
>
> "So many innocent teenagers go through this same kind of thing and many end their own lives because of the ignorance out in the world. I mean, if high school is like this, what is the rest of the world like?"—Robert, 15

Ideas That Can Get You Down

It's okay to feel depressed sometimes. That's natural. Here are some common thoughts that can lead to depression, and some advice on what can help you feel better:

I am the only GLBTQ person in the entire world.

Feeling like you're the only one can really bring you down. In fact, the most commonly accepted statistics say that roughly one out of every ten people is gay, lesbian, bisexual, or transgender. With all of the billions of people in this world, that's a whole lot of queer folks.

> **BEEN THERE**
>
> "I had my youth group to go to every Tuesday night when I was in high school. I had three adults to talk to if I ever needed something from them and I had the whole group. We would discuss our problems and get advice from each other on what we could do to help our situations."—Sonia, 19

There is something wrong with being GLBTQ.

Maybe you feel that it's wrong to be GLBTQ and that queer people are somehow bad. But being queer is completely natural, and it doesn't make you wrong or bad or mentally ill. There are a lot of medical and mental health groups that say the same thing. In case you're wondering who they are, they include:

- the American Academy of Pediatrics
- the American Counseling Association
- the American Psychiatric Association
- the National Association of School Psychologists
- the National Association of Social Workers

These groups collectively represent nearly half a million health and mental health professionals, and they all maintain that queerness is not a mental disorder. That's almost half a million people who think you're just fine.

I can never have a normal life.

GLBTQ people can live the most "normal" of lives no matter what your definition of that might be. We can be and are doctors, lawyers, politicians, construction workers, artists, teachers, parents, counselors, executives, factory workers . . . anything we want to be. We can be single or have a partner. We can have families. We can own homes. In our lifetimes, we experience joys and sorrows, love and heartbreak, pleasure and pain just like anyone else.

I'm popular and I have friends. I should be happy, but I'm not.

Even if you're popular or get good grades or your home life's fine, it doesn't necessarily mean that your life is easy. When you're trying to understand your sexual orientation or gender identity, you can feel like you're alone and out-of-sync with the rest of the world, even if everything looks good from the outside.

Most mental health experts agree that the source of some people's depression may have little to do with outside factors. Instead, their depression is related to imbalances in the chemicals in the brain that regulate their moods. Some people may be more prone to depression if it runs in their family.

Everybody hates me because I'm GLBTQ.

The truth is, many people care about you and a lot of people just don't give a hoot whether you're GLBTQ or straight. The following numbers may give you a positive perspective:

- According to GLSEN, 83 percent of parents support putting in place or expanding school anti-harassment policies to include GLBTQ teens.

- According to the National Gay and Lesbian Task Force (NGLTF), 83 percent of people in the United States support equal rights in employment for GLBTQ people and 75 percent support equal rights in housing.

Warning Signs of Depression

From the outside, other people like parents and teachers may not be quick to recognize depression because it can look like the normal and sometimes difficult feelings that teens wrestle with every day. You may have a better chance of figuring out if you're depressed more so than the people around you, so it's important to be aware of how you're feeling, thinking, and acting. Many of the following changes can be normal in adolescence. The difference in depression is that they are extreme, even painful, changes in the way you feel and behave and they might last a long time. If you're experiencing any of the following for more than two weeks, you could be depressed:

Emotional changes such as:

- anger
- guilt
- anxiety
- feeling numb
- hopelessness
- irritability
- indifference
- loneliness
- sadness
- bitterness
- feeling worthless
- feeling helpless

Physical changes such as:

- sleeping problems (too much or too little)
- overeating or loss of appetite (often with weight gain or loss)
- headaches
- indigestion, stomachaches, or nausea
- aches or pains for unknown reasons
- fatigue, lack of energy, lack of motivation

Thinking changes such as:

- difficulty remembering or concentrating
- confusion
- believing that no one cares about you
- loss of interest in things you used to enjoy
- pessimism (negative thinking about everything)
- believing that you don't deserve to be happy
- believing that you're a burden to others
- blaming yourself for anything that goes wrong
- thoughts racing through your head
- thoughts of harming yourself
- thoughts of death or suicide

If you're feeling suicidal or thinking about hurting yourself...

...please talk to someone *right away*. A trusted adult, a crisis line, or a good friend can help you get through this crisis time. (See the resources that follow for a list of crisis lines.)

Behavior changes such as:

- aggression
- moving and talking more slowly
- poor hygiene
- acting out (skipping school, driving too fast, running away, taking part in unsafe sexual behaviors)
- abusing drugs, alcohol, or nicotine

- crying more than usual
- underachieving or overachieving
- spending most of your time alone and withdrawing from friends or family
- hurting yourself (cutting or burning yourself, for example)

The previous checklists were adapted from *When Nothing Matters Anymore* by Bev Cobain (see page 208).

If you're depressed, a lot of resources and people are available to help you. *If at any time you feel like hurting yourself or feel suicidal, you need to get help immediately.*

RESOURCE

Depression and Suicide Prevention

Here are some crisis lines that can help you now *and* connect you with additional resources in your area:

A GLBTQ Helpline

The Trevor Helpline: 1-866-488-7386
The Trevor Helpline is a 24-hour toll-free suicide hotline for GLBTQ youth and teens. They also have a Web site at *www.thetrevorproject.org*

continued——▶

with information about how to help someone who is suicidal, as well as support groups and resources for GLBTQ teens.

General Crisis Lines

The Girls and Boys Town National Hotline: 1-800-448-3000
This crisis hotline for teens is available 24 hours a day. Professional counselors listen and offer advice on any issue, including depression, suicide, and identity struggles.

The National Hopeline Network: 1-800-784-2433
This network is for people who are depressed or suicidal, or who are concerned about someone who is. The line connects callers to the nearest certified and available Crisis Center, where trained counselors answer 24 hours a day, 7 days a week. You should reach a trained counselor in 20 to 30 seconds and never get a busy signal or voicemail.

National Runaway Switchboard: 1-800-786-2929
This is a toll-free, 24-hour hotline that provides confidential crisis intervention for a variety of issues, including depression and suicide and referrals for teens and their families. They can help connect you with counseling services in your area.

You can use the crisis lines in this book or you can look in your phone book for a local resource. In a special front or center section of your local yellow pages, you should find services including crisis, depression, or suicide hotlines listed under a heading such as "crisis," "mental health," "depression," or "suicide." (You can also look for listings in the body of the yellow pages.) Using those same search words, you can also search the Internet for crisis lines, counselors, and organizations that can help you.

There's nothing wrong with turning to another person for help. It doesn't mean that there's something wrong with *you,* but that there's something wrong *in your life.*

Making a Deal for Life

Make a deal with a person you trust—whether it's a friend, parent, or someone else—that, if you're ever feeling really low, you can call him and he'll be there for you to talk to any time, day or night. And, likewise, you'll be there for him, too. It can make you feel so much better to know you will always have someone to lean on.

We, _____ and _____ ,
[insert your name]   [insert your friends name]
hereby swear that we will henceforth, from
here on out, and into infinity be there for one
another. We know that, at any hour of the day
or night, if we need to talk, we can call and the
other will listen. Also, we swear that if we ever
have thoughts of doing ourselves harm, we will
call the other person for help.

Signed:

Person #1 _____

Date _____

Person #2 _____

Date _____

Thinking About Drinking:
Making Decisions About Alcohol

Being a teen means making a lot of tough decisions about alcohol, nicotine, and other drugs. It's your body, and those choices are yours to make. You'll have to live with the outcomes, so it's in your best interest to make the most informed decisions possible.

While overall use of alcohol, drugs, and tobacco has declined somewhat for teens, substance abuse rates are higher for GLBTQ teens than for their straight peers. A lot higher. According to a 1999 article in the *Journal of Consulting and Clinical Psychology,* GLBTQ teens are 50 percent more likely to use alcohol, three times more likely to use marijuana, and eight times more likely to use crack cocaine.

Why do queer teens have higher rates of alcohol and drug abuse? The process of realizing and accepting that you're GLBTQ can be incredibly stressful, especially when it's combined with the general everyday stresses of being a teenager. The verbal and sometimes physical harassment that many queer teens deal with daily can increase stress levels, too. That much stress can lead to depression, which can lead to substance use as a way to feel better. Many teens look for ways to escape their stress and worries and turn to alcohol and drugs, thinking those will cheer them up, mellow them out, help them fit in, or at least numb them.

BEEN THERE

"Drugs and alcohol can be a problem for many GLBTQ men and women. It makes us feel temporarily like our problems are gone and life is great, but the truth about it is the more you do the worse you feel, and life is just gonna get worse. Relationships fall apart from it and people get hurt."—Ben, 18

A Gay Old Time? The Party Scene in GLBTQ Life

Some people believe the stereotypes that all or even the majority of GLBTQ people drink, smoke, and use drugs. While the bar and club scene does have its place in GLBTQ culture, the idea that all queer people party and use substances is far from true. Bars and clubs, however, may be the first or most obvious places that teens find out about when they start looking for signs of the GLBTQ community. As a result, GLBTQ teens may find themselves where drugs are more common simply because they're looking for community or a place where they can fit in.

In an interview for GayHealth.com, Michele Fitzsimmons, out-reach coordinator for the Lesbian AIDS Project said that GLBTQ youth tend to gravitate toward queer bars and clubs because they're some of the only places where they feel comfortable expressing their sexuality. "When you're coming out, your self-esteem might be shaky," she says. "It's very easy to slip into a situation where [drug and alcohol use] becomes an addiction or that use puts the user at risk."

If you're at a place in your life where you're looking and may even be desperate for acceptance, it's easy to find yourself doing things like drinking to fit in, taking ecstasy (X) to relax, or smoking to strike up conversations. The drugs, alcohol, and tobacco found at clubs may be tempting, but not all GLBTQ people who go to clubs drink, smoke, or use drugs. It's not a requirement to fit in.

Other options exist, but if you do decide bars and clubs are where you want to go to meet people, it will help to plan in advance how you're going to handle the pressure, temptation, or opportunity to use substances. Be aware that there are people in clubs who aren't thinking clearly. If you want to stay safe and have a positive experience, your best bet is to keep a clear head. For example, if you want something to drink, get it yourself. Don't let someone who you don't know very well bring you anything to drink. No matter how nice she may seem, she could easily slip a substance such as Rohypnol, Ketamine, or GHB into it.

The Truth About Drinking

In the United States, turning 21 is considered a huge right of passage. It's the magical age when you suddenly understand how to drink responsibly, you've crossed the finish line—the wait is over, so drink up! It's not surprising that people get the idea that drinking is a wonderful thing and they can't wait to try it. Think of how much pressure that puts on people and what messages that sends about alcohol. It's easy to forget that alcohol is a drug that can cause a lot of problems.

Many people—and not just teens—have misconceptions about how alcohol works and what it will do for them. Here are some of the more common myths:

When you're feeling stressed or depressed, having a drink will make everything feel better.

GLBTQ teens do have a lot to deal with, but alcohol, instead of helping you forget your problems, can actually compound them. Alcohol is a depressant that slows down your brain, making it easier to get depressed and harder to think things through clearly. It might seem like it's giving you a lift, but it's actually bringing you down.

Drinking makes you cool.

Lots of people are lured by the idea that drinking will make them look cooler and more mature. For GLBTQ teens, the idea that drinking can help them fit in, whether they're at a high school party or an over-21 club, can be attractive, especially if they're feeling like outsiders. But alcohol won't suddenly help someone become popular or fit in. Drinking can actually create the wrong impression.

Drinking will help you meet people.

Meeting people while under the influence of alcohol or other drugs is not the way to put your best foot forward. If you're looking for meaningful relationships and new queer friends, you won't come across as your best self if you're tipsy, high, or flat-out drunk. Drinking also can seriously impair your judgment, which means you could say or do embarrassing things, things you wouldn't ever do when you're sober. Or you could end up making decisions about things like having sex or drinking and driving that you might regret and that you wouldn't have made otherwise.

BEEN THERE

"During the nine months that I was drinking, I didn't meet one person who I knew was gay. Once I could stop drinking, I made several gay friends and, ultimately, started to date again. Although I came out to my father and to all my friends when I was 16, it was almost like coming out again once I stopped drinking, because of all the people I met and of coming to terms again with who I am."—Blake, 20

Ways to Say No to Alcohol

You can say no to drinking without feeling awkward, self-conscious, or like a prude. By saying no to drinking, you're looking out for yourself and being self-confident. Still, the pressure to drink can sometimes feel overwhelming. If you're having trouble saying no, here are some tips that may help:

- Order a drink, but order a club soda and lime or something else nonalcoholic.

- If someone asks you if you want a drink, just say, "No, thanks," or hold up your club soda and say, "I've got one."

- Say, "I want to go dance instead."

- Be a designated driver.

- Be supportive of friends who choose not to drink.

RESOURCE

Getting Help

If you have or think you might have a drug or alcohol problem, get help. Call the National Council on Alcoholism and Drug Dependence at 1-800-622-2255 or visit their Web site at *www.ncadd.org*. You can also contact the National Association of Lesbian and Gay Addiction Professionals (NALGAP) for information or a referral. Call (703) 465-0539 (a toll call outside of the Northern Virginia area) or visit them online at *www.nalgap.org*.

The Truth About Tobacco

If you look at the statistics, you're more likely as a GLBTQ teen to use tobacco than your straight counterparts. According to the Centers for Disease Control (CDC), 59 percent of GLBTQ teens reported using tobacco as opposed to 35 percent of straight teens. If you start using tobacco when you're a teen, chances are you'll continue to use it as you grow older. According to a Surgeon General's report, 88 percent of people who smoke had their first cigarette by age 18. This shows that teens are very popular with tobacco companies.

If you open one of your favorite magazines, like a music magazine for example, it's a good bet that you'll see a cigarette ad. The message of the ad is probably that it's cool to smoke. Think about who develops the ads—the tobacco industry, a group of companies that make their money from getting people addicted to something that can kill them. Now think about who they're targeting—*you.*

Documents from the tobacco industry were made public as a result of the 1998 Master Settlement Agreement, which settled numerous law suits against the tobacco companies for billions of dollars. These documents consistently show that big tobacco targets teens with their marketing messages. They also targeted gays with a marketing project called "Project Sub Culture Urban Marketing," known inside the major tobacco company RJ Reynolds as "Project S.C.U.M."

The Truth

For more information on how the tobacco industry lures teens, the real effects of tobacco on your body, and more, visit the Web site for The Truth, a group dedicated to educating teens about all aspects of tobacco, from health effects to the overall industry. The Truth is located at *www.thetruth.com.*

Getting Hooked on Tobacco

You can pick up the habit by hanging out in cafes, clubs, or other places where a lot of people smoke. If you're feeling isolated or eager to meet others, smoking can seem like a social link or a way to approach others. Some people like to use lines like, "Got a light?" or "Can I bum a smoke?" when they want to meet someone.

There's a powerful and addictive chemical in tobacco called nicotine, which can make smoking easy to start, but hard to stop. Nicotine provides smokers with what can feel like a great fix. However, studies have shown that nicotine is actually more addictive than heroin. Nicotine cravings can be so intense that people are willing to stand outside in sub-zero weather just to get some.

GLBTQ teens sometimes turn to smoking as a release from their daily stresses, a way to relax, or as a way to relieve some of the depression they might feel. Tobacco may give a temporary feeling of relief, but it is only temporary and it comes at a cost—increased heart rate, decreased stamina, weaker lungs, and increased risk of developing cancer. According to the CDC, tobacco kills more people than AIDS, murder, suicide, fires, alcohol, and all illegal drugs combined.

Dealing with Drugs

Just as with alcohol and tobacco, GLBTQ teens have a higher rate of drug use than straight teens. It's not that queer teens are fundamentally prone to substance abuse. It all comes down to stress and depression. Like some GLBTQ teens who drink or smoke because they think it will take the edge off, make them feel better, or help them fit in, others turn to drugs for the same reasons. In the end, drugs don't work any better than drinking or smoking. They don't help you escape or change a difficult situation.

> **BEEN THERE**
> "I started doing drugs when I was nine, trying to fit in with that crowd and also to hide my 'secret identity.' By the time I was 13, I was put in drug rehab. . . . My rehab counselor told me I wasn't going to be able to stop using unless I was true to myself. I went home and thought about it that night, and the next day I started coming out to friends, but you know how that goes—one person knows, the whole city knows."—Sam, 15

Instead of solving problems, drugs compound them. When you're depressed, many drugs may make you feel a little better at first but then, as their effects wear off, much worse (similar to the effects of alcohol). If you're feeling really stressed, drugs that are supposed to make you happy often leave you feeling paranoid, jittery, or out of control. In general, drugs are pretty unpredictable. You don't really know what you're getting and you can't be sure how they're going to make *you* feel.

If you like to go out dancing or to raves, it's likely you'll come across drugs like ecstasy (X), ketamine (Special K), LSD, or GHB. These can be just as dangerous and unpredictable as any other drugs. It's tempting to think they'll help you forget about the teasing at school or the fight you had with your parents about your girlfriend, or they'll just put you in the mood to do some serious dancing. It doesn't always work that way, even with "club drugs." According to the Partnership for a Drug Free America, the number of ecstasy-related emergency room visits among teens has risen ten-fold since 1995.

RESOURCE

Educate Yourself

To find out more about the different kinds of drugs and their effects, from alcohol to X, or to read postings from teens about drug use, visit the Partnership for a Drug Free America Web site at *www.drugfree.org*. For more information, including stories from other teens about their experiences, check out *www.freevibe.com*.

Even if you're not using drugs yourself, someone else's drug use could get you into serious trouble. Never ride with someone who is drunk or high, even if she swears to you that she's sober. If you have a license, offer to drive her somewhere. But even if she refuses, don't get in the car with her. If you do, you're putting your life in her hands.

The rule of thumb with drugs is: no chemically induced high is without a hitch. For anything drugs give you, they take something else away. And what they take is a lot more valuable to you in the long run than the high they give you in the short run.

No matter what anyone may tell you, no matter what stress or depression might make you think, you have the potential to make anything you want out of yourself; you can do amazing things with your life. If you need help, reach out for it. It's there and it's never too late.

> **BEEN THERE**
>
> "I remember shooting up a mixture of heroin and cocaine, and what happened next really scared me to the point of not wanting to touch drugs and alcohol again. I was 20 and I was down on my knees in the middle of the night, blood pouring out of my nose, throwing up, and I just remember praying that if I woke from this that I would never touch drugs again. I was very lucky during that time when I was using drugs that I did not catch anything, that I wasn't raped, or that I didn't kill anyone else or myself."—Lee, 26

Getting Clean as a GLBTQ Teen (and Staying That Way!)

If you're using drugs or alcohol, quitting could be one of the most difficult things you ever do in your life, especially if you're still coming to terms with issues related to being GLBTQ. Even though it's challenging, getting clean will also be one of the most positive things you can do, and it's a crucial step to getting yourself back on track.

No matter what forces are working against you (your dad can't accept that you're queer, you're being harassed at school, you're feeling isolated), you do have the power to change your life. No matter what is going on outside of you, there is a whole lot of strength inside of you. You *can* stay clean.

Here's some advice on how to get sober and stay clean:

Recognize that you have a problem.

If you don't see the problem, you can't solve it.

Get help.

The support of your parents, your friends, or your doctor can be of great help when you quit drinking or using. If you can't approach your parents about your problem with drugs or alcohol, seek the support of another adult you know well and trust. Talk with your guidance counselor, your favorite teacher, a relative, a religious leader, a doctor, or another caring adult. It doesn't matter who it is. What's important is that someone knows about your problem and can be there to help. This can be tough because it will involve coming out to whomever you talk with, but you can do it. You are worth it.

Keep in mind why you're trying to quit.

Getting clean will not be easy. It helps, though, to remember the benefits of overcoming addiction. You'll feel better both physically and mentally. And conquering drugs and alcohol will make you a stronger person than you probably thought you could be.

After you've stopped drinking or taking drugs, the hard part can be staying clean. Here are some things that may help you:

Once you start a treatment program, tell your friends about your decision to stop using drugs.

Your true friends will respect and support your decision. It is possible that you'll have to find a new group of friends who are completely supportive of your efforts to stay sober. Avoid hanging out with people you did drugs or drank with before if they continue to drink or use. Don't get pulled back into old habits or behaviors.

Let your friends and family know how important their support is and ask them to be there for you when you need them.

It's important that you have someone you can call in the middle of the night if you need someone to talk with. Even if you don't end up calling, knowing someone is there can be very comforting.

Only accept invitations to events that you know (or are at least reasonably certain) won't involve drinking or drugs.

Especially when you're first recovering, it's safer to avoid situations where you'll be tempted to drink or use drugs.

Know in advance what you'll do in situations where you are exposed to drugs or alcohol.

You'll likely be tempted to start using or drinking again, but knowing beforehand how you'll approach difficult situations will make them easier to deal with. Your plan might be as simple as "get the heck out of there." Even so, if you know what to do in advance, it's easier to follow through and take care of yourself when you need to.

Always remember that having an addiction doesn't make you a bad or weak person.

If you slip up in your efforts to stay clean, get help as soon as possible. But remember how difficult what you're doing is and know that there's nothing to be ashamed of. You've made a lot of positive changes in your life and one mistake doesn't change that.

> **BEEN THERE**
> "As I complete six years clean and sober, I have just begun finding out who I really am. Now I find myself surrounded by men and women whose friendship I am thankful for everyday."—Lee, 26

9 RELIGION AND CULTURE

Hate is not a family value.

There are many different aspects that make up who you are as a person. Sexuality is an important part of the whole, but religion, culture, and ethnicity also play an important part in your day-to-day life. They influence how you see yourself and how others see you in society. If you were raised with strong religious or cultural beliefs, coming to terms with your gender identity or sexual orientation might leave you feeling confused about who you are or where you belong.

Some people have trouble accepting themselves as GLBTQ—or have trouble gaining acceptance from loved ones—because of religious beliefs and cultural traditions. The roots of religion and culture can run very deep, and anything that challenges those beliefs can be met with resistance and even anger. This can make it hard to understand yourself, or for others like family and friends to understand you. Accepting yourself and coming out is even more stressful if you feel like you have to choose between your cultural or ethnic identity and being GLBTQ.

Religion and culture sometimes are difficult to separate as influences because religion can play such a key role in defining a culture's beliefs and traditions. For example, Catholicism is often an integral part of both Latino and Filipino cultures. Islam is influential in cultures around the world from the Middle East to parts of Asia and the Pacific Rim. The Christian faith is often considered a cornerstone of African-American culture.

If your religion teaches that it's wrong to be GLBTQ, that belief may surface throughout the culture, not just inside the temple, church, or mosque. It's not surprising that you may find yourself with conflicted emotions. On one hand, you want to come to terms with your sexuality and to learn to accept yourself. On the other hand, you've grown up as part of a religion or culture that teaches that who you are is not okay. So now what?

States of Being: Religious Life and GLBTQ Life

For many families with GLBTQ loved ones, religion can be a huge challenge to reconcile. For others, it's not an issue at all, either because they do not practice a religion or their religion or faith community is openly accepting of GLBTQ people. Then there are those in the middle—GLBTQ people whose families accept them, but their religions do not.

Note: In this chapter, congregation is used to mean a gathering of people for the purposes of religious worship or instruction. It is not used to refer to a specific faith, and it is used interchangeably with religious community, faith community, and place of worship.

Religion is important in many people's lives and that may be true for you, too. In the United States and many other countries, it is very common to grow up in a family that practices some kind of organized religion. According to a 1995 Gallup Poll, 71 percent of Americans responded that they were members of a church or synagogue.

On the surface, religion and sexuality don't seem to have much to do with each other. Being GLBTQ is about your sexual orientation or gender identity—the result of a combination of biological and emotional factors. Religion is about spiritual beliefs. So why is religion such a complicated and even painful issue for many GLBTQ people?

A History Lesson

Many major religions have difficulty accepting or finding a place for their GLBTQ members for various reasons. They can be scriptural, historical, rooted in cultural traditions that have become part of religious beliefs, or a combination of these factors. One reason is the belief that a union between a man and a woman is sacred.

A strong, positive, and loving relationship between two people is definitely something to celebrate. However, the idea that the union between a man and a woman is sacred is often because the couple can reproduce. In fact, there are some religions that believe that a couple should have sexual intercourse only for the purpose of reproduction, period. As a result, GLBTQ people can find themselves, their sexuality, and their relationships rejected by their religion, because reproduction isn't the primary purpose of their romantic and physical relationships.

Encouraging Open Minds: Starting a Dialogue

Knowledge can be your best path to finding acceptance and understanding in your religious community. When people start looking at where their personal beliefs and their religion's beliefs come from, it can get them thinking. The question, "Why do we believe this?" may seem simple, but people can be afraid to explore or challenge their own belief systems, often because they're scared that what they discover about some of their beliefs may end up invalidating all of them.

If you are struggling with your religion, find out about its history and where anti-GLBTQ beliefs might have originated. Read the original writings or scriptures to get a better idea of how others have interpreted them. An issue or idea can be taken out of context and personal opinions can influence interpretations.

A Research Project

If you want to find out more about your religion's history but aren't sure where to start, an Internet or library search could be a good jumping-off point. If you feel comfortable doing so, approach a religious leader in your community and ask for recommendations, or your congregation might have its own library. Some of these sources may be biased, but some of them could provide solid historical information and discussion. Also, many queer-positive religious organizations have lists of resources and suggested reading lists. (See pages 151–153 for a list of the these organizations.)

If you have a loved one who's struggling with these issues, talk with her about what you've learned. She might not be willing to listen, or she might sit down and really consider the information. Investigating your religion's roots and starting a dialogue are positive steps toward reconciling who you are with your religious beliefs. If you're at a loss as to how to approach family, friends, or people in your religious community, refer back to the coming out chapter for tips on effective communication. Much of that advice is appropriate for approaching a wide variety of topics that can be difficult to discuss.

BEEN THERE

"My mother struggled with religious issues above all else. It was very difficult for her for a long while, but then she found a book called *Prayers for Bobby* by Leroy Aarons, which changed the way she felt almost overnight."—Robert, 15

Room for Change

Many religious communities are engaged in debates about their queer members. These debates may include whether or not to accept GLBTQ members, specific conditions under which GLBTQ members are allowed to be part of the congregation, and whether or not to perform commitment ceremonies. While some religions may never accept GLBTQ people, the fact that so many are finally thinking and talking about it is very encouraging. Even if the end decision by a religion's leaders is to not accept GLBTQ people, the debates themselves help open and change individual minds.

It can be very discouraging to hear that a group of religious leaders has officially decided not to welcome GLBTQ people. Try not to think about it in terms of an entire organization, because there are going to be people who disagree and who *do* accept GLBTQ people.

Making Room in Religion:
Reconciling Your Personal Beliefs

Religion and culture can be very personal, meaningful aspects of a person's life, and that doesn't have to change because you're queer. You may find a place for yourself in your religion, in a different spiritual tradition, or follow your spiritual beliefs as an individual rather than as part of a group.

> **BEEN THERE**
> "I don't consider myself as having a religious background because organized religion is not the way for me to go. I consider myself a very spiritual person without the aspect of religion. Religion doesn't affect me either way, at least not on a level I notice. I know that learning that I'm GLBTQ would affect my family—grandparents and great-grandparents—very negatively. They can't see beyond the religion."—Elena, 20

Here are some common questions and answers that may help you figure out what's best for you right now:

Q: What do I do if my place of worship doesn't accept GLBTQ people?

A: First, are you sure that queer people are not welcome at your place of worship or have you made that assumption on your own? Have you been taught that it is wrong to be GLBTQ, or do you assume your congregation isn't accepting either because nothing has been said about it or because you don't know of any other GLBTQ members?

Whatever the case, you might want to approach the leader of your congregation to explore her views on having GLBTQ members. If one or both of your parents is accepting, perhaps they could accompany you. Your religious leader may be willing to explore the issue with you and the two of you can grow together. Then perhaps, the entire congregation could move toward becoming more open and accepting.

Just as accepting yourself and coming out is a process, so is change. Give your religious leader and community a chance. Even if they're not willing to be affirming of GLBTQ people at first, they may be willing to learn more about what it means to be queer. There are several national organizations whose members are willing to visit places of worship to talk with the leader or congregation about becoming more open and accepting.

RESOURCE

GLBTQ-Positive Religious Organizations and Resources

PFLAG *(www.pflag.org)* and the Human Rights Campaign *(www.hrc.org)* are both good places to look for basic information and resources. If you're interested in finding queer-positive groups and information about your religion or denomination, the following list can help get you started.

www.affirmation.org
Affirmation is an organization for queer Mormons and their Web site has a Youth Section with information about queer Latter Day Saints youth groups and a variety of other information and resources.

continued——▶

www.al-fatiha.org
The Al-Fatiha Foundation is dedicated to GLBTQ Muslims and their allies, families, and friends. Their Web site hosts several discussion groups, and the information section has a list of group chapters, resources and links, and writings.

www.dignityusa.org
Dignity USA is a large, progressive organization for GLBTQ Catholics and their friends. Its resources include a list of local chapters, materials for queer teens and their parents, and materials in Spanish.

www.gaybuddhist.org
This site has information about Buddhism and meditation, news of interest to queer Buddhists, and a helpful Spiritual links section with links to resources, practice groups, and organizations.

www.gaychristian.net
This site's goals are to provide resources to queer Christians including links to churches, organizations, and books, and to bring Christians together for encouragement and prayer.

www.integrityusa.org
This is an inclusive organization for GLBTQ Episcopalians and their friends, which advocates for their full inclusion in the Episcopal Church and equal access to its rites. The site contains information about local chapters and diocesan networks and how to get involved.

www.interfaithalliance.org
The Interfaith Alliance is a nonpartisan, clergy-led grassroots organization with members from 65 different faith traditions. It promotes the positive role of faith in civic life and challenges intolerance. It has been active in lobbying for GLBTQ civil rights.

www.jqyouth.org
This Web site is specifically for GLBTQ youth from a variety of Jewish traditions, including Modern Orthodox and Conservative Standard. While this social/support group is based in New York, it has members

continued——▶

from all over the world because of its online discussion group, helpful FAQs, and resources (including a list of related organizations around the world).

www.OrthoGays.com
A site for queer Orthodox Jews, it has FAQs and information about and links to many articles, resources, and organizations.

www.pflagphoenix.org/resources/religious.html
The PFLAG chapter in Phoenix, Arizona, has a wonderful list of links to a wide variety of GLBTQ-positive religious organizations and Web sites. There are groups for Buddhists, Muslims, Jews, Pagans, and a diverse assortment of Christian denominations including Quakers, Baptists, Methodists, Seventh Day Adventists, Jehovah's Witnesses, Mennonites, and Pentecostals.

www.soulforce.org
Soulforce is an interfaith group that applies the principles of non-violence to stopping "spiritual violence"—inflammatory and false misinformation about GLBTQ people used to deny them their rights or cause them harm. The site has a list of local chapters and a wide variety of resources about GLBTQ issues and religion.

www.ufmcc.com
This is the Web site for the Fellowship of Metropolitan Community Churches. These churches have a special focus on the GLBTQ community and have been active in protesting intolerance and hate crimes against GLBTQ people. The site has resources, online classes, and discussions of various Bible passages often used against GLBTQ people. Many resources are available in different languages including Spanish, Russian, and Chinese.

Q: What if my religious community won't accept me?

A: Unfortunately, some religious communities and congregations won't be willing to change. But even if yours is one of them, don't assume that you will be forced to abandon your religion. You may be surprised to learn that, in almost every religion, there are branches or denominations that are accepting of GLBTQ people. In virtually every religion, the key religious texts (for example the Bible, Torah, or

Koran) are interpreted in a variety of ways. Some interpretations are more conservative, others are more liberal or inclusive. Your particular place of worship may welcome only straight people, but another place within your religion may be more open and accepting.

How welcoming or open a place of worship is to queer people can depend on a number of different factors: where you live, the congregation's familiarity with GLBTQ people, how diverse the congregation is, the individual beliefs of the community's spiritual leader.

Some people choose to stay with their original congregation but continue to work for change. Others opt to stay in their congregation and reconcile themselves to the idea that their congregation won't change. There is no right or wrong decision. Religion is a very personal issue and only you can decide what's best for you.

BEEN THERE

"I'm Lutheran. Some people may not realize that there are basically two different Lutheran churches, the Evangelical Lutheran Church of America (ELCA) and the Lutheran Church, Missouri Synod (LCMS). One is very liberal, and the other is more hellfire and damnation. . . . There is a push in the ELCA church to allow GLBTQ pastors to be ordained and in committed relationships. In the past, you could only be ordained if you were straight or, as a GLBTQ person, chose celibacy. There are those who grew up LCMS, like my mother, who are not so accepting."—Charlotte, 19

You may be in a situation that for now makes it difficult or impossible for you to attend a different place of worship. Maybe you're too young to drive or you simply don't have access to transportation. For these or other reasons, you may have to wait a while to make changes. Remember, there is nothing wrong with you. You deserve as many opportunities and as much happiness as anyone else in the world. Continue to explore your religion and look for ways to find your place in it despite the views of your congregation or religious leader.

Q: What if I can't find another congregation within my religion that is open and accepting?

A: You might be able to find a different denomination, or branch, within your religion that holds similar beliefs and has a more accepting congregation in your area. For example, Christianity has many denominations. They all work within the same basic belief system and use the same religious texts (the Bible), but they may have different interpretations, views on issues, and practices. Some denominations have a lot in common, some less. You may be able to find a congregation within a similar denomination which would be comfortable for you.

If there is no other denomination similar to yours, or if there is not an accepting faith community within a similar denomination close to you, you may have to look at other options. You may even want to consider joining a completely different (instead of similar) denomination or exploring other spiritual practices and traditions.

Some spiritual communities like the Unitarian Universalists welcome everyone. These communities may have members who are Jewish, Buddhist, Muslim, Christian, or who don't subscribe to a particular religious focus, all within the same congregation. The worship services are conducted in such a way that all beliefs are respected. While this could be a big change from the way you're used to worshipping, you can always visit once or even a few times to see what you think. You might love it and decide to stay, or you might feel that it's not the right choice for you.

Q: None of these options works for me. What can I do?

A: You *still* have more options. Some GLBTQ people decide that they can't, at least at this point in their lives, reconcile their sexual orientation or gender identity with organized religion. While the prospect may be scary for you if you've grown up with a strong religious background, it may help to remember that religion is about exploration. Give yourself the opportunity to explore what is right for you.

You may explore other religious traditions and find one that's more accepting and feels like a better fit. You may move to a new denomination, or you may eventually end up some place where you find an accepting religious community in your original denomination. Religion is very personal and you might also opt to practice it on your own. You may find that practicing your religion or exploring your spirituality in a more personal way and outside of a formal setting helps you clarify what you believe.

Remember, whatever decision you make now doesn't have to be permanent. You can change your mind. You may decide that you need to leave organized religion, and eventually decide that religion doesn't have a place in your life at all. Or you may maintain your religious practices or explore your spiritual beliefs as an individual, instead of as part of an organization.

> **BEEN THERE**
>
> "Around 14 or 15, I got deeply religious, bought myself a Bible, and began attending church regularly and went to study groups and nightly Bible classes. I suppose I was trying to make it work, since everyone assumed I would get into it if I just tried harder. But in the end, it just never worked. It wasn't for me. . . . When I think about the specifics, it's like everything I do and the things I like are all wrong, and I'm bad. But I'm NOT! I'm not bad, so the problem is elsewhere. Since then, I've explored a number of different religions and spiritualities."—Renée, 19

The decision to leave organized religion, change religions, or to practice on your own might be upsetting to your family. Talking to them about it calmly and rationally may help, especially if you explain how and why you made your decision. You may choose to add that you're not closing yourself off to religion, you're just taking another path, at least for now. You might come back, you might not.

Some parents or guardians respect such decisions. Others do not. If you're living at home, you might be in a situation where you must still attend your family's choice of religious services. Even if you hear anti-queer messages at these services, try not to take them to heart. These messages are often the result of fear and ignorance. Not everyone in your religion believes them and neither should you. Know that you are a good, kind person who is just as worthy as anyone else in your faith community.

Q: I grew up dreaming about a wedding. Do I have to give that up?

A: There are many GLBTQ people who celebrate special occasions such as weddings and other religious or cultural rituals and traditions. They do this either by holding their own private ceremonies or by holding ceremonies within open and accepting religious communities.

Same-sex marriages aren't legally recognized yet in most countries, including the United States (though domestic partnerships are legal in some countries in Europe, including Denmark, Hungary, Sweden, and the Netherlands). Instead, many queer people hold their own ceremonies, often called "commitment ceremonies," to express their love for and commitment to one another.

Can't We Be Married in Vermont?

In 2000, Vermont made civil unions for same-sex couples legal, because its state Supreme Court ruled that gay and lesbian couples were due the same protections, benefits, and obligations that straight couples received with marriage. While civil unions are an important step forward and have most of the state-sponsored protections and benefits, they aren't exactly the same as marriages. For example, the rights of same-sex couples "married" in Vermont don't have to be recognized in any other state.

Having a commitment ceremony doesn't mean that one person will have to wear the tux and the other a dress, although you can do that if you want. A commitment ceremony can be however you want. It can be like a traditional wedding, take place in the woods or on a beach, or be in your parents' backyard. It's up to you and your partner.

Q: I'm fine with my religion. What can I do to help others who are struggling?

A: If you have been able to reconcile your religious or spiritual beliefs with your sexual orientation or gender identity, you have a tremendous opportunity to help others. It doesn't matter whether it was easy for you or the result of intense soul searching. Many people have a tough time accepting themselves because of their religious backgrounds or beliefs. Sharing your experiences with them can provide the encouragement and help they may need on their own journeys.

You could become part of, or even form, an outreach group within your own congregation. Such groups offer those who are struggling an opportunity to talk with and hear from others who have had similar experiences. You could also look into working with an interfaith alliance that deals with issues related to GLBTQ people. They offer many opportunities to volunteer. You can also join or start an Internet chat group for those who are struggling with religious issues.

Cultural Differences, Being GLBTQ, and You

Cultural traditions, like religious ones, may be a big part of your day-to-day life. Culture is made up of many things—race or ethnicity, religion, where you were born or raised, the language(s) you speak. Specifically, it may influence family traditions, how and what holidays you celebrate, nicknames, what language you speak at home or with friends, music, and food. Culture can also be a strong influence on gender expectations and sex roles such as how you're supposed to behave, dress, and talk as well as who you're supposed to date.

Reconciling your cultural and family traditions with the need to understand and accept your sexuality or gender identity can be a complex and sometimes painful process. You might feel like you're being called to choose one identity or the other and that you aren't allowed to be queer *and* a person of color, for example. To make matters more complicated, GLBTQ people who belong to ethnic, racial, or social minorities are viewed as having "two strikes" (or more) against them in society. They may face discrimination for being queer and they may also face discrimination for being African American, Asian, Latino, Pacific Islander, Arab, or Native American.

> **BEEN THERE**
>
> "I was born in Singapore. Until recently, I had not understood cultural differences from a theoretical perspective. Instead, I recognized cultural differences through my own experiences as a queer woman of color. My innate understanding of cultural differences left me unable to integrate all parts of my identity in certain spaces. For example, being half Asian and half Caucasian, it is often difficult to integrate my Asian identity when in the company of only white peers. In virtually all spaces, my queer identity is not integrated or even understood."—Adrian, 20

Part of the struggle can be invisibility. You may feel like your culture doesn't have a place in it for GLBTQ people. You might also feel isolated or invisible in the queer community, if you aren't seeing anyone else in it with a similar background. Role models, community, and seeing yourself reflected in the society around you are important factors in accepting yourself.

RESOURCE

For GLBTQ Teens of Color

There are many groups and Web sites for queer people of color to help them connect and discuss common issues and concerns. (Some of the religion resources on pages 151–153 may also contain helpful resources in their links or information sections.)

www.youthresource.com/living/youth_of_color.htm
This section of the Youth Resource: LGBT Youth of Color site is devoted to issues specific to queer teens of color. Each ethnicity, including Native American and cross-cultural, has its own subsection with first-person stories and resource lists that include books, articles, Web sites, and organizations. This site as a whole (*www.youthresource.com*) is very inclusive and contains information helpful to and perspectives from queer teens of color.

continued———➤

www.ambientejoven.org
Ambiente Joven is completely in Spanish for GLBTQ Latino teens and young adults. It has lists of organizations and community resources throughout the United States and South America, links to other sites of interest, and information on religion, sexuality, and safer sex.

www.glaad.org/poc
The Gay & Lesbian Alliance Against Defamation's (GLAAD) People of Color Media Program is dedicated to promoting fair and inclusive representations of GLBT people of color. The Web site contains articles and resources specific to various GLBT communities including those of African, Asian Pacific, and Latino/a descent. Sign up for their newsletter to receive news updates specific to your community of color.

www.nyacyouth.org
The National Youth Advocacy Coalition site has a wide variety of resources for Latino, African-American, Cross-cultural, and Asian/Pacific Islander queer teens. They also have information about their anti-racism and racial and economic justice initiatives.

www.trikone.org
Trikone is a nonprofit organization for GLBTQ people of South Asian descent (including people from Afghanistan, Bangladesh, Bhutan, India, Maldives, Myanmar, Nepal, Pakistan, Sri Lanka, and Tibet). Its goal is to bring people of South Asian heritage together, affirm South Asian identity as well as GLBTQ sexual orientation and gender identity, and fight discrimination.

No matter where you're from or what your ethnic background, there have been and are queer people in your culture. How they've been viewed and treated varies widely. Some GLBTQ people find that their racial or ethnic backgrounds make being GLBTQ, or at least being out, difficult for them.

This can be for many reasons. For some, it is because many of their cultural traditions are tied to religious beliefs. For others, it's because being GLBTQ is seen as going against strongly held cultural beliefs about sex roles and how gender is expressed. In some cultures, being GLBTQ is seen as undermining the family by not carrying on the family name or going against family expectations. Coming out can be difficult in many cultures because it's seen as embarrassing or bringing shame on the family (or even on the race) because it makes public something that is considered to be private.

These influences can form some powerful barriers to understanding and accepting GLBTQ people. Unfortunately, many queer people of color may feel isolated from their communities for these reasons.

> **BEEN THERE**
>
> "Being an African-American woman has made it more difficult to be GLBTQ. Then people make it an issue as well that I'm a lesbian and black and I won't succeed because of those factors combined. I know who I am, and my culture and its negativity just make me a bit stronger, because there is nothing worse than being ostracized by people you can identify with on many issues except this one. I've grown to not care how they feel about it because it doesn't matter how they feel, as long as I love myself."—Elena, 20

The traditions of other groups have a different effect. Some Native American cultures, for example, have a history of recognizing and accepting their GLBTQ members. Navajos have a word for people who are considered neither men nor women—*nadle*. The Lakota also had words to describe males and females who lived outside of typical gender roles—*winkte* and *koskalaka*. The Omahas had a word that meant either someone who is neither male nor female, or for a transformation from a man or a woman to a different gender—*mexoga*. Certain societies didn't just accept transgender people, but even looked at them with reverence.

> **BEEN THERE**
>
> "To address the issue of my heritage, I do identify with my Cherokee heritage. As does anything, it has shaped my character, but in small ways. My heritage and my sexuality were never at odds with each other."—Scott, 19

More Cultural Factors

While religion and culture have a strong impact on personal identity, many other factors can affect how society sees you and how you see yourself, both as an individual and as a queer person. Resolving identity issues can be challenging for GLBTQ people. It can be all the more challenging for queer people who, for example, have disabilities, have a chronic illness, are from low-income families, aren't average-sized—you can probably think of plenty of other things that can make a person stand out from the crowd.

Anyone who does not fit in with what society calls "norms" (but what are actually just "averages") and who is also GLBTQ could be dealing with issues of identity, fitting in, and feeling invisible (or too visible) on many levels. Just as there are norms in society, there are norms within the GLBTQ community that can lead you to have expectations about who's queer and what queerness looks like. If your school has a GSA, think for a moment about all the different people who are members. You all may have a lot in common, but there are probably plenty of differences, too. And those differences, whether they're disabilities, economic background, or something else entirely, may leave you wondering where you fit in or confronting GLBTQ as well as society's norms.

For example, maybe you're in a wheelchair. Were people surprised to see you at the meeting because they'd never thought about someone being disabled *and* queer before? You might face a similar reaction if the situation were the other way around and you came out at the meeting of a disabled students group. (Or maybe you were the person who was surprised.) This is just one example of what it can be like to try to figure out who you are and to be yourself in two very different communities.

It can be a complicated process, but diversity is a positive thing. It enriches our lives and the lives of those around us. If you think of yourself as a mosaic, and each aspect of who you are as one more colored tile, you will see that each color contributes to creating the intricate and beautiful picture of who you are.

Being a Whole Person: Reconciling All Parts of Yourself

If you're having a hard time reconciling your culture, religion, or disability with being GLBTQ, you may feel alone, confused, or scared. Figuring out where you fit in your culture as a GLBTQ person and how it fits into you can be a long process. It can help to remember that there are GLBTQ members of every race, religion, ethnicity, and cultural group. No matter who you are, you're not alone.

It may help to talk with other GLBTQ people with similar backgrounds or heritages. If you are struggling with issues such as those related to race, ethnicity, and religion, talk to someone about it. Depending on where you live, there may be support groups available. If not, the Internet can be a great place to touch base with people who understand what you're going through.

10 TRANSGENDER TEENS

There is no choice in being yourself.

"Since I was little I would always lay awake at night and wonder how much better my life would be if I had been born a girl, but then I would think 'Oh, great, the one thing I really want, I can't have.'"—Alexandra, 14

In many ways, transgender (or trans) teens have an even greater struggle for acceptance and understanding than other queer teens. Very little is known and understood about what it means to be transgender, so trans teens can face even greater feelings of isolation and loneliness than their gay, lesbian, and bisexual peers. "Our society hasn't even begun to deal with transgender issues," Michael Ferrera, clinical director of group homes for the organization Gay and Lesbian Adolescent Services, told Human Rights Watch in a 1999 interview. "Transgender teens are experiencing things no one has begun to consider."

Unfortunately, there isn't much research on transgender teens. While there is a rough idea of how many gay, lesbian, or bisexual teens there are, the same information doesn't exist about teens who identify as transgender. In 2001, Human Rights Watch released a report on GLBTQ students in school called *Hatred in the Hallways,* where they stated, "No definitive data on the prevalence of people who identify as transgender exist."

This lack of information about transgender teens, and trans people in general, means that society is still very much in the dark about what it means to be transgender. Even in the medical community it can be difficult to find mental health professionals and physicians who are capable of providing educated, compassionate care for trans people.

But this lack of understanding doesn't mean there is something wrong with you. It means that society has been slow to learn. But it will. Transgender people are becoming more visible and will continue to do so. If you are transgender or if you think you might be, it's important to reach out and seek help. Despite a general lack of understanding in society, you are *not* alone and there *are* resources for you. Groups like the National Transgender Advocacy Coalition are fighting for your rights.

What Does It Mean to Be Transgender?

When you're transgender you have a gender identity or gender expression that is different from your biological sex or physical anatomy. A few definitions may be helpful here. *Gender identity* is your internal sense of being male or female—it's whether you consider or feel yourself to be male or female. Your *gender expression* is how you express your gender identity and includes the clothes you wear, your hairstyle, and your body language (how you walk, your posture, your gestures). In society, people often take their cues from someone's gender expression to decide that person's anatomical sex.

Transgender is a broad term that covers many different groups. It includes transsexuals (in all stages), crossdressers, drag kings and queens, and people who are intersex, among many others (see the following Q&A or the glossary for definitions of these terms). People who are trans may identify themselves in a variety of ways. (For more about self-describing and its importance, see pages 170–171.)

What it *feels* like to be transgender is different for every person. Many TG, or trans, people describe feeling "trapped in the wrong body." Others describe it more as having an internal sense of self that isn't reflected on the outside by their bodies.

> **BEEN THERE**
>
> "From a very early age I knew I was different. I always preferred dressing up as a princess rather than a police officer or a fireman. This carried on through my childhood, and into my teenage years whereby I became increasingly frustrated about not being able to be the girl I wanted to be. When I came out to my parents, I explained that I never felt right as a male, and that I have always wanted to be a girl."—Alycia, 19

TG Q&A

You may have a lot of questions about what it means to be transgender. If you do, you're not alone. While the GLBTQ community as a whole is working for greater visibility and more rights, gay, lesbian, and bisexual people tend to receive more recognition and acceptance than trans people. As a result, it's still common for people to lack a basic understanding of general issues that relate to being transgender. This can be true even in the queer community.

Here are some common questions and answers about being transgender:

Q: Why are people TG?

A: According to PFLAG, many in the scientific community believe that being transgender is the result of complicated biological factors that are determined by the time someone's born. This means that you don't suddenly become transgender and that you don't choose to be transgender—you are born a trans person.

Q: Is being transgender a mental disorder?

A: The mental health community labels the transgender experience as *gender dysphoria*—a term for the pain, anxiety, and confusion that can result when a person's gender identity and biological sex don't match. The pressure to conform to accepted gender roles and expression and a general lack of acceptance from society also contribute to gender dysphoria.

Mental health professionals often diagnose transgender people with *gender identity disorder* (GID). Transgender activist Jessica Xavier explains that some transgender people struggle with the advantages and disadvantages of being diagnosed with GID. A diagnosis of GID lets transgender people get mental and physical treatment, which can be especially helpful for people trying to physically transition their gender. The flip side of a GID diagnosis can be the stigma of being diagnosed with a mental disorder—people and medical professionals may treat transgender people like they're sick or mentally ill.

Q: Do all TG people want to have surgery to change their anatomies?

A: No. In an effort to deal with their gender dysphoria, many trans people go through a period of *gender transition*. During this time, they begin to change their appearances, and often their bodies, to match their gender identities. This might mean that they start wearing clothing different from that of their birth sex and change hairstyles. People may also work on changing how they walk and move at this time and even the sound of their voice. Some people undergo minor cosmetic procedures such as electrolysis (permanent body hair removal) as well.

Gender transition doesn't necessarily include surgery. It is a misconception that all transgender people want to change their anatomies through *sex reassignment surgery (SRS)*. Sex reassignment surgery modifies primary sex characteristics (the genitals) and is sometimes accompanied by surgeries on secondary sex characteristics as well (breasts, Adam's apple). People who don't identify with the sex they were born and who may change their bodies through hormones and surgery to reconcile their gender identity and physical sex are referred to as *transsexuals*. (All transsexuals are considered transgender, but not all transgender people are transsexual.)

Nonoperative transsexuals may not be interested in or able to have surgery. They may or may not take hormones as part of their transition process. Some trans people take hormones and go no further in their physical transition. Others are preoperative transsexuals, who may be in the process of transition and haven't had sex reassignment surgery, but plan to. Others are postoperative transsexuals, which means they have had the hormone therapy and the various surgeries needed to complete a total physical transition. Surgery is an option that is usually restricted to those over the age of 18.

Q: What does intersex mean?

A: Some people are born intersexed, which means they were born with both male and female genitals or with ambiguous genitalia. Some intersex people have surgeries, often in infancy and throughout their childhood, to definitively assign them one anatomical sex. The surgery doesn't always result in a physical sex assignment that matches the person's internal gender. As a result, some intersex people grow up with gender identity issues that mirror those experienced by transgender people.

Q: Who are crossdressers?

A: Crossdressers are people who dress in clothing of the opposite sex. They may do this in private or try to pass as the opposite sex in public. Crossdressers used to be called transvestites. They can be male or female and can be straight, gay, lesbian, or bisexual.

Q: Are transgender people also gay, lesbian, or bisexual?

A: Some are, but many are not. It's a common misconception that transgender people are all gay, lesbian, or bisexual. In fact, many trans people are straight. Some trans people are assumed to be lesbian or gay because of their gender expression.

However, some straight trans people may at first come out as gay, lesbian, or bisexual, while they're trying to figure out their gender identities. Even though they have a different gender identity, they're attracted to persons of the same anatomical sex but they haven't considered the possibility of being transgender. For other people who later realize that they are transgender, they initially take their feelings of being the opposite anatomical sex to mean that they're gay or lesbian. This is probably because gay and lesbian people are more visible in society than transgender people. It might not occur to a teen that he is transgender because he's never seen any transgender people to identify with.

> **BEEN THERE**
> "I passed a period of my life going out with other girls, as lesbian. But something didn't quite feel right. I've always wanted to be a guy, physically."—Kevin, 18

Q: If many transgender people are straight, why are they often lumped together with gay, lesbian, and bisexual people?

A: Transgender people share much of the same struggle for acceptance and recognition as gay, lesbian, and bisexual people. The issues of gender expression and sexual orientation often overlap. Frequently anti-queer bias and behavior has a lot to do with gender expression rather than sexual orientation.

For example, a female who wears her hair short and prefers to wear traditionally male clothing may get teased and harassed or called a lesbian, because she's stepping outside her traditional gender role. She may be lesbian or bisexual, or she may be transgender, or she may just like having short hair and wearing more masculine clothing.

People aren't reacting to her sexual orientation, they're responding to her gender expression. Some people feel threatened or afraid and may discriminate or get angry when they see people expressing their gender in untraditional ways. GLB and trans people both often face this same discrimination when they don't conform to other people's ideas of gender.

Historically, transgender people have even faced discrimination from the gay, lesbian, and bisexual communities because of a lack of understanding about trans issues and an unwillingness to work together for greater acceptance for all GLBTQ people. One of the great things about GLBTQ teens today is your overall willingness to be inclusive and not draw strong lines between what it means to be gay, lesbian, bisexual, or transgender.

Describing Your Gender Identity

Since transgender is a blanket term that covers several distinct but related groups of people including transsexuals and crossdressers, self-description can be really important to transgender people. Trans people often use a variety of different terms to describe themselves, or self-identify.

> **BEEN THERE**
> "I came out at 15 as a lesbian but later I was trying to figure out if I was a boy or a girl. I changed my name from a girl's name to a boy's in order to see how it would feel. I loved looking at boys and their muscles and also women and their muscles. That's what I wanted. The ability to have that. But I couldn't. Finally, at 25, I really took the time to try and figure it all out. If I have to identify at all, it is as a butch lesbian, but I don't want to have to live within only those parameters."—Lee, 26

There is some debate in the trans community about what terms can be applied to who. For example, some postoperative transsexuals—those who have taken hormones and had surgery to more accurately reflect their gender identity—don't call themselves transsexual. As far as they're concerned, they've become the opposite sex.

In the end, it's a very personal decision, and no one but the individual can choose how to self-identify. From transgender, female-to-male (FTM), male-to-female (MTF) to gender queer, gender neutral, and multi-gender, the only thing that matters about the way you identify is that it's both comfortable and meaningful for you.

Two- Spirit People

Many Native American tribes had special words, and even held reverence, for people who today would be characterized as transgender. Certain Native American cultures described transgender people as having "two spirits." Generally, Two-Spirited people were born into one sex but took on the gender roles for both sexes (though this definition varies some across cultures). Two-Spirited people were often revered as healers, peacemakers, and shamans. Today, some transgender people identify as "Two Spirit."

How Do You Know?
Figuring Out If You're Transgender

As with figuring out if you're gay, lesbian, or bisexual, self-discovery is a process. Maybe you've felt like someone of the opposite sex for as long as you can remember, or maybe you've had a vague feeling of being different that you can't really define. You might arrive at the conclusion that you're transgender relatively easily, or it could take months or years to figure out.

There isn't a checklist that can clearly indicate if you're transgender, but transgender people do tend to share some common experiences. Perhaps some of these are familiar to you:

1. Have you ever felt that there is a conflict between your body and your mind?

According to a 1997 article in *The International Journal of Transgenderism,* trans people often report a disconnect or conflict between their minds and bodies, sometimes to the extent that they feel they were actually born with the wrong anatomy or into the wrong bodies.

As you grow up, especially as you go through puberty, it's common to have some feelings of gender confusion. That doesn't necessarily mean that you're transgender, or even gay, lesbian, or bisexual. Part of being a teen is defining yourself. Exploring gender roles is a natural part of figuring out who you are.

> **BEEN THERE**
> "When I was a kid, everyone else seemed to know they were boys or girls or men or women. That's something I have never known; not then, not today. As a kid, I just figured I was the crazy one; I was the one who really had some serious defect."—Writer/ Performer Kate Bornstein, from *Gender Outlaw: On Men, Women, and the Rest of Us*

2. Do you dislike or avoid activities and interests that are usually associated with people of your birth sex?

Dr. Milton Diamond writes that many trans people describe disliking and avoiding activities that are traditionally associated with people of their anatomical sex and strongly preferring activities and behaviors that are traditionally linked with their preferred sex. Often these likes, dislikes, and ways of behaving are obvious from an early age. For example, a young boy might enjoy playing with girls rather than roughhousing with other boys and hate football, avoiding it in favor of playing dress-up and experimenting with his mother's makeup.

A word of caution: Being uncomfortable with traditional gender roles doesn't necessarily mean that a person is transgender. Many young children try a wide variety of activities and behaviors regardless of which biological sex they're usually associated with and they don't turn out to be transgender. In the case of most transgender people, however, it goes beyond exploring and they are expressing very strong, almost overpowering, feelings with their interests and behaviors.

You Go Girls: Challenging Gender Roles in History

In early 18th century Germany, a woman named Catharine Margaretha Linck dressed as a man, served in the army, then went to work as a cotton dyer. Catharine even married a woman (although the bond wouldn't have been legal). During the Revolutionary War, Deborah Sampson dressed as a man and joined the Continental Army. Deborah was also known to have romantic relationships with other women.

3. Do you have thoughts of wanting to be the opposite physical sex?

It's one thing to occasionally have a thought like, "Life would be easier if I were a guy." It's another to have a constant desire to be the opposite sex.

> **BEEN THERE**
> "I've always been fascinated with the idea of being a girl, I guess. I used to watch this show about a boy who suddenly acquires the ability to become a girl when he comes into contact with hot water. I could never really understand, though, why he was so very distressed about being a girl."—Chris, 19

4. Do you identify strongly with the experiences of people who are transgender?

One way to explore your gender identity is to find out more about transgender people. It can be helpful to read about their experiences or talk with others who identify as transgender. You may find that while people use different language to describe their experiences, their actual experiences and feelings are similar. If you have a lot of gender feelings and experiences in common with the people you're talking to or reading about, it could mean that you are transgender as well.

RESOURCE

Read All About It

TransProud, a Web site for trans teens at *www.transproud.com,* has posted at their site a collection of stories from teens of all ages and genders about realizing they were trans, how and if they came out, and how they live their lives. (Many of the quotes in this chapter came from the TransProud Web site.)

BEEN THERE

"It's hard to say definitely how I became aware of my gender identity. I think it was really while I was surfing some Web sites and reading stories about transsexual people that I realized not all guys have dreams of suddenly and inexplicably being changed into a girl, or fantasize about growing breasts."—Chris, 19

Now What? Options for Trans Teens

What do you do after you realize you're transgender? This is a complex question, and it's one that has many potential answers. You may wait and think about things. You may come out as transgender. You may decide to change your name or start dressing differently, and possibly start transitioning socially into your gender identity. Or you may decide that you need a complete physical transition and start looking into sex reassignment surgery. There are many decisions to make.

But the first thing you'll need to do is accept yourself as a transgender person. This can be very difficult for some people. Being a transgender person doesn't mean there's something wrong with you, although it may feel that way. It is part of who you are and there is nothing wrong with that. It may take time to come to terms with being transgender and you may need help to work through what being trans means for your future.

Coping with Negative Emotions

Realizing that you are transgender may leave you feeling confused, lonely, scared, and worried about what your future will hold. How will being transgender impact your family, future romantic relationships, and even your future career? But just because you've realized and accepted that you're transgender doesn't mean that your process is over. According to PFLAG, unlike gay, lesbian, and bisexual people who feel conflicted largely as a result of an emotional dilemma, trans people feel conflicted because of a physical dilemma. A disparity between gender identity and physical self can create an ongoing struggle.

That continuing struggle can have devastating emotional effects, particularly if the TG person believes there's no hope for change or progress. According to the Washington Transgender Needs Assessment Survey conducted from 1998–2000, transgender teens are at greater risk for committing suicide. Over 16 percent of those surveyed had attempted suicide and far more had thought of it. That's almost twice the national average for teens overall.

Because you are working through complicated emotional and identity issues, it's important to take care of yourself. Here are some ways to get started:

Get support.

Support could come from a friend, parent, sibling, teacher, school counselor, mental health professional, or someone else. Support needs to be nonjudgmental. Talk with one person or several people who will listen to you without downplaying your feelings. Also, the person or people you talk to should not try to persuade you to conform or to deny your feelings of being transgender.

If you don't feel comfortable talking with anyone you know, don't give up. There are many sources of support available to you. In addition to national organizations, there are local groups and Internet sites for transgender people to receive support, encouragement, and advice. Many of these Web sites also have email lists or forums where you can talk with other transgender people.

Seek counseling.

Transgender activist Jessica Xavier advises trans people to seek counseling, not because there is something wrong with being transgender or because you should try to change, but because it's a way to get the support you need. Therapy should be aimed at helping you understand, accept, and feel good about your personal identity. (If your counselor tries to convince you to deny your gender identity or conform, get help from someone else.) It's common to be uncomfortable about gender issues. It can be easy to internalize fears about trans people and to believe there's something wrong with you. A skilled counselor can help you deal with these kinds of feelings and ideas.

Find a counselor who is knowledgeable about transgender issues. A good place to start is a local or national GLBTQ or trans organization.

RESOURCE

Organizations for Transgender People

Gender Education and Advocacy (GEA) at *www.gender.org*
This site is filled with news, information, and resources for the transgender community. You can search the resources by state to get a list of local support groups, therapists, places to safely socialize, and even places to shop in your area. There are also resources for families and partners of trans people, a list of gender programs, information about Medicaid, and resources for intersex people.

Gender Public Advocacy Coalition (GenderPAC)
1743 Connecticut Avenue NW, 4th floor
Washington, DC 20009
(202) 462-6610 (a toll call outside the Washington, DC, area)
www.gpac.org
gpac@gpac.org
A gender rights advocacy group, GenderPAC's site contains news and the latest legal information. Violence prevention, public education, and workplace fairness issues are addressed, and there's also a section specifically for youth that includes information on activism, TG youth news, and a school violence survey.

continued➞

International Foundation for Gender Education (IFGE)
P.O. Box 540229
Waltham, MA 02454
(781) 899-2212 (a toll call outside the Waltham, MA, area)
www.ifge.org
info@ifge.org
IFGE is a transgender advocacy and educational organization. It maintains a bookstore and publishes a magazine on transgender issues. It also provides telephone referrals. The Web site has a wide variety of links and information.

National Transgender Advocacy Coalition (NTAC)
P.O. Box 76027
Washington, DC 20013
www.ntac.org
info@ntac.org
NTAC advocates for full civil rights for all transgender and intersex people in all areas of society. It actively protests incidences of discrimination. Their Web site contains news, legal information, and a list of transgender links.

The PFLAG Transgender Network
at *pflag.org/tnet.tnet.0.html*
This trans, PFLAG-affiliated site has resources and links and a wonderful booklet, *Our Trans Children,* which can be read online or downloaded as a PDF. This booklet, written by transgender activists, is full of detailed and useful information as well as dozens of resources.

TransFamily at *www.transfamily.org*
This site supports transgender and transsexual people and their families and loved ones. In addition to resources, links, and information, there are email discussion lists, a "letters to loved ones" section, and newsletters.

Trans*topia
at *www.youthresource.com/living/trans.htm*
This transgender section of the Youth Resource Web site contains firsthand accounts by transgender teens and young adults, resources (books, organizations, and Web sites), and a series of articles about emerging medical issues, how to select a therapist, and how to keep yourself safe and healthy.

Coming Out

Often one of the first steps you may take after you realize you're transgender is to come out. It may only be to a few close friends or family members, or it may be to a lot of people. This is particularly important if you want to start living in a way that better reflects your gender identity. Transgender people who wish to transition their genders by living full or part time in their new gender are usually forced to come out because the transition is so obvious.

Coming out—whatever the circumstances—can be a stressful process for everyone involved. And just like coming out as gay, lesbian, or bisexual, the people you're coming out to may be accepting or they may be confused, sad, or angry. (It may help you to refer to chapter 3 for ideas about how to come out.)

According to Jessica Xavier and PFLAG, parents, especially, may have serious difficulties dealing with their children coming out as transgender. Some parents feel they're losing a son or daughter. When a teen tells her parents that she wants to live her life as someone of a different gender, her parents might experience symptoms of grief similar to death—a feeling that the daughter they raised has suddenly been taken from them.

The people you come out to may not understand what it means to be transgender and may have lots of questions for you. It can be very difficult for your parents and other people who care about you to learn that you have been struggling with such a tough issue. They may worry about you and your future. However, they may also want to help and support you.

> **BEEN THERE**
>
> "It was the most nerve racking thing I have ever done. I had my doubts, but I had made up my mind it had to be done. They were shocked, as I expected, but they seemed to be happy that I'd told them. We talked about the possibilities for me for hours, and eventually they agreed that as long as I'm happy, they'd support me in whatever I wanted to do."—Alycia, 19
>
> *continued*➞

"I accidentally came out when my dad saw some pages I'd been looking at on the Internet. My dad eventually just said 'So, let's talk about
what you look at on the Internet.' This was my cue to explain to him
everything. He asked lots of questions. He was very curious about me.
He had done an amazing amount of research on the Internet himself.
He looked up sex reassignment surgery doctors, he looked up how
much the procedure would cost. He looked up all that he could on
hormones, and he had even contacted an M2F [male to female trans
person] through the Internet to see if he could find out anything
that might help me out. It did. It helped me out immensely just to
know that there is someone who cares about me."—Amanda, 18

When you come out, it's important to let your family and loved
ones know that there are resources available to help them, too. (See
pages 176–177 for a list of transgender resources.) Many national
transgender organizations will help you find local support either
through their Web sites or with phone referrals. Your local phone
directory may list additional resources. PFLAG also offers services for
trans people and their families and friends, including a brochure titled
Our Trans Children.

Changing Names

One of the first things many transgender people choose to do is
change their name to one that better reflects their gender identity. As
a teen, you can't legally change your name without your parents' consent. But some teens do change their names in practice, asking their
families and friends to use their new names.

Changing your name to one that reflects who you are can be a positive means of asserting your true identity. It can sometimes be difficult to get people to take your name change seriously or to accept it.
Some parents, friends, and school administrators will be very supportive and accepting. Others will reject the idea completely.

If you are certain that you are transgender and you're thinking
about changing your name, here are some things to consider:

Come out first.

Telling your family and friends that you're transgender and, in the same breath, asking them to call you by a different name is a lot for people to process. It's likely that they'll have a lot of questions about what it means to be transgender, and if you can help them understand that, then you can help them get to a place where they'll understand why you feel the need to change your name. However, if your parents seem fairly receptive to your coming out, you might want to discuss your name of choice. It's up to you, but be sure to take it one step at a time, and allow your family and friends to do the same.

Try to be patient.

Some people will be respectful of your request to use your new name. Others will not. Even those who are respectful will probably need time to get used to the change.

According to clinical psychologist Dr. Sandy Loiterstein, many transgender people report that their name change was very difficult for their parents to accept. She explains that a child wanting to change his name can have deep emotional implications for the parents. They might see it as a rejection of something very personal they have given to their son or daughter. Changing names can also deepen the grieving process that many parents of transgender people go through, because it can emphasize the idea of loss to them.

If your parents are struggling, it can help if your family speaks with a therapist knowledgeable about transgender issues. This can help them understand the issues you're facing and help your entire family learn how to deal with your transgender identity.

Choose your name carefully.

Put some thought into your new name. Choose a name that's representative of your personality or meaningful for you in some way. Also, it's usually a good idea to choose a somewhat conventional name. If you ask people to call you something like Fabulosa, chances are they won't take you seriously.

Some transgender people choose names are that are feminine or masculine versions of their birth names. So Sam becomes Samantha and Charlotte becomes Charles. Others choose gender-neutral names, such as Alex. Or they might choose another name entirely.

If you want to change the name you use at school, get your parents' support.

It can be extremely difficult to get teachers and staff to use your new name at school, even with your parents' support, much less without it. But having your parents behind you can help when you're talking with your principal, school counselor, or teachers. Sometimes changing your name at school is easier if you're starting at a different school or in a different grade. People may have less to associate with your previous name.

Some transgender teens choose to use their birth names at school (or have to if their school refuses to use their new name) and use their chosen names at other times, depending on who they're with (family and friends) and where they are (at home or in public). And some trans teens decide to wait until they're older to change their names, either legally or in everyday life.

Gender Transitioning

For some people, changing their name is the first step in gender transitioning. Gender transitioning is a complex, multi-step process of starting to live full time as a person of a different gender. Transitioning doesn't, by definition, include surgery or other physical changes, though it may involve those things depending on the person. It primarily involves social issues such as changing your name, dressing differently, altering other aspects of your appearance like hair or makeup, and changing your mannerisms, voice, and how you move.

Gender transitioning can also involve many physical changes for some trans people. A physical transition may include taking hormones or other substances, under the supervision of a medical professional. For some, transitioning may also include surgery. Surgery is an option almost always reserved for adults. As a transgender teen it is very unlikely you can undergo sex reassignment surgery, although you might be able to work with an endocrinologist who can assist you with hormone treatments. It is rare to find a physician willing to prescribe hormones to someone under 18, but there are some who will.

> **BEEN THERE**
>
> "Perhaps it all began when I was but a child, six years, maybe, watching Saturday morning cartoons—specifically, Bugs Bunny donning a dress and a wig. I was enthralled at the transformation. This, I decided, was what I would aspire to. That's as far back as I can recall about my 'difference.'"—Zelia, 15

Physical Transitioning

Undergoing a physical gender transition can be a long and complex process. For some transgender people who wish to undergo a full physical change, it can be a vital process and one that holds great reward. There are many steps and professionals involved and some services can be extremely difficult for those under 18 to obtain. It is extremely rare that minors are allowed to undergo full physical transitions. Sex reassignment surgeries are also very expensive, and many people spend years saving to afford them.

The physical transitioning process takes a long time for many reasons. Some physical changes take months and sometimes even a few years to complete. But the physical changes for transition must be supervised by medical professionals who can help you explore your feelings and decisions, as well as help guide you through the process.

If you want to transition, especially if you want to pursue sex reassignment surgery (SRS), you'll need to know about the Standards of Care. These are guidelines that were created by the Harry Benjamin International Gender Dysphoria Association. They are the standards under which most trans people obtain hormone therapy and SRS. There are relatively few surgeons who perform SRS, and most, if not all of them, follow these standards.

The Standards of Care include a period of psychotherapy in order to confirm that a person is truly a trans person, the beginning of hormone therapy (which is a lifelong process), the administration of the Real Life Test (living full time as the intended gender for a period of time), and finally, if desired, SRS.

Typically, a period of psychotherapy is required *before* a person begins taking hormones. The therapy and assessment period can last for three months or longer, depending on the mental health professional and the person receiving treatment. Young people often feel like the validity of their transgender identity is being questioned, or feel like the people assessing them think that because they're young, they're only going through a phase or overreacting. It can be frustrating to feel like others are second-guessing something you're very certain about. Try to release those negative feelings in a positive way, like writing about them in a journal. (For more tips on releasing negative feelings, check out chapter 2 on homophobia and transphobia.)

BEEN THERE

"I think the most difficult part of being transgender is the way my gender identity and my body just don't match. It's a constant source of frustration and annoyance for me. I'm not currently on hormones because I have not had enough counseling yet. One of the things that annoys me most is the attitude of protecting a young transsexual from him/herself."—Chris, 19

The Real Life Test is a period (a minimum of one year) during which a transitioning person must live and work, if he is in the work world, full time as someone of the sex that matches his gender identity. In other words, a female-to-male (FTM) would have to live as a man for a minimum of one year. This test is monitored by medical professionals.

Only after the successful completion of the Real Life Test (as determined by the supervising physician) can a person become a candidate for SRS. The sex reassignment surgery involves the permanent refashioning of the sexual anatomy. Beyond genital surgery, many transgender people undergo additional procedures. MTF people may have facial and body hair removed, an operation to reduce the size of the Adam's apple, and various cosmetic surgeries to achieve a more feminine-looking face and body. Some MTF transsexuals may also have breast augmentation surgery, though many just rely on their hormone treatments to develop breasts. FTM transsexuals may have their breasts removed in addition to surgery on their genitalia. Even with these procedures, being able to pass as your new physical sex isn't guaranteed. Some people never pass completely. However, many do.

Some teens who get impatient with the transitioning process or who find it difficult to obtain hormones from a doctor, buy hormones on the street. Buying hormones on the street can have serious negative physical and legal consequences. Taking street hormones is risky and you're breaking the law. As with drugs, hormones bought on the street could contain anything and their strength and dosage is unknown. Hormones should be taken under a doctor's supervision, preferably an endocrinologist (a doctor who specializes in hormones) and at the proper dosage, which can vary from person to person. If you are under 18, you might have to wait to obtain hormone treatment legally.

Trans Pride: Responding to Transphobia

Transphobia is still very common because gender roles tend to be so deeply rooted in many societies. The general lack of understanding about what it means to be transgender can make it difficult for trans people to find acceptance from their families, in school, and from society as a whole. Transphobia can lead to name-calling and discrimination and escalate into harassment and even violent attacks.

Just as with homophobia, you can respond to transphobia in many different ways—by ignoring it, speaking up, attempting to educate people, or getting involved in working for change. However, be very careful to assess the situation before deciding how to respond. According to Human Rights Watch, trans students and others who challenge traditional gender roles in more obvious ways often endure the greatest harassment and some of the worst physical attacks. While safety is a big concern for gay, lesbian, and bisexual students, it is a *huge* concern for transgender students.

If you are being harassed at school and you're not getting support from administrators, teachers, or other adults, you can get help.

Organizations such as GLSEN, NGLTF, and the ACLU will all help you fight discrimination in your school. There are transgender and gender rights advocacy groups that can help, too. (See the resources on pages 176–177 or at the end of this book for contact information for these groups.)

Facing Discrimination

Social pressures to conform to gender stereotypes can be extreme. Because gender expression is so visible and obvious, it's easy to find yourself facing unwanted attention or harassment. TG people who are transitioning or those who can't *pass* (live relatively unnoticed as a different sex) can be especially vulnerable to harassment and even physical abuse. Unfortunately, there are few

legal protections for trans people and, in recent cases, the courts have found that trans people are not covered by existing anti-discrimination laws even if those laws protect people based on their sex or sexual orientation. Some states, counties, and cities do offer protections for transgender people. To get information on the most current legislation, visit the Human Rights Campaign (HRC) Web site at *www.hrc.org.*

Just as with gay, lesbian, and bisexual people, discrimination against and abuse of trans people is *never* okay and it is never justifiable. If you have been attacked, report the attack to the police. If the police refuse to recognize your claim or file a report, a national organization like Lambda Legal *(www.lambdalegal.org)*, the National Gay and Lesbian Task Force *(www.thetaskforce.org)*, or the ACLU *(www.aclu.org)* may be able to help. There are many transgender groups like GenderPAC *(www.gpac.org)*, the National Transgender Advocacy Coalition *(www.ntac.org)*, and Gender Advocacy and Education *(www.gender.org)* who can also help you. These organizations advocate for trans people and lobby for their legal rights. You do not have to suffer alone or in silence.

Trans people can also face discrimination at work, in part because the transition process is so readily apparent. Transgender activists are also working overtime to get an amendment added to the Employment Non-Discrimination Act (ENDA) before Congress votes on it. This Act and amendment would make discrimination in the workplace based on sexual orientation or gender identity illegal. (For more on ENDA, see page 192.)

In spite of the harsh discrimination many trans people face, increasing numbers of people are coming out as transgender, and that increased visibility will help educate others about what it means to be transgender. Being a trans person can present some difficult issues, but many trans people live very meaningful, fulfilled, and happy lives. The most important thing you can do is learn to accept yourself for the wonderful person that you are.

Ⅱ WORK, COLLEGE, AND BEYOND

Life, liberty, and the pursuit of happiness are not "special rights."

Many teens enter the working world during high school. For others, college comes first and work and careers are something they plan to address afterwards. Either way, if you're GLBTQ, entering the work force or choosing a college can present special challenges, for example, figuring out whether you want to be out at work or finding a GLBTQ-friendly college.

Finding a GLBTQ-Friendly Company

Some teens aren't concerned about their employer being GLBTQ-friendly. For others, it's very important. Either way, it's helpful to know where you stand. Increasing numbers of public and private employers are including sexual orientation in their nondiscrimination policies. Unfortunately, far fewer include gender identity.

Employers tend to be open to prospective and current employees about their human resources policies. You should be able to find out fairly easily whether a company has a nondiscrimination policy. You can search its Web site or ask a company representative. An employee handbook should also contain information about the company's nondiscrimination policy. Many companies post their policies in lunch or break rooms, print them on job applications, or hand out copies automatically with any other employment-related paperwork.

The Human Rights Campaign (HRC) offers a service called WorkNet. WorkNet has resources and articles about GLBTQ issues in the workplace. It also has a section devoted specifically to transgender issues. One of its most helpful features is an employer database that lets you search for companies that include GLBTQ people in their nondiscrimination policies, offer domestic partner benefits, or have queer employee groups, among other options. The WorkNet database is located at the HRC Web site at *www.hrc.org*. HRC sends a survey on GLBTQ issues to major companies to gather information that is pub-

lished each year in the *Corporate Equality Index.*

According to HRC, currently there are almost 5,800 employers that offer domestic partner benefits in the United States. This includes 177 state and local governments and 189 Fortune 500 companies who have adopted domestic partner benefits since Washington, D.C., enacted its law recognizing domestic partners of District employees in 1992.

The

13

Most GLBTQ-Friendly Companies

According to the Human Rights Campaign (HRC), the following employers received a perfect score on the HRC *Corporate Equality Index 2002*. (The companies were judged on seven criteria that included whether the company has nondiscrimination policies for sexual orientation and gender identity, domestic partner benefits, and diversity training that includes GLBTQ issues.) These are the friendliest of the GLBTQ-friendly companies:

Aetna Inc.	Lucent Technologies Inc.
AMR Corp./American Airlines	NCR Corp.
Apple Computer Inc.	Nike Inc.
Avaya Inc.	Replacements Ltd.
Eastman Kodak Co.	Worldspan L.P.
Intel Corp.	Xerox Corp.
J.P. Morgan Chase & Co.	

Eighty-one companies received the next best score of 86 percent, which means they met six of HRC's seven criteria. These companies included Bank of America, IBM, Levi Strauss & Co., Starbucks, Target, and Walt Disney.

Being GLBTQ in the Workplace:
Your Decisions and Your Rights

People approach being GLBTQ in the workplace in many different ways. Some people prefer to keep that they are GLBTQ private, or don't bring it up unless it happens to come up by itself. Others feel it's important to have coworkers know they are GLBTQ. There's no right or wrong way to address this issue. It's based largely on what you prefer or what you feel comfortable with.

Should I Tell a Prospective Employer I'm GLBTQ?

Often queer people wonder whether they should come out to a potential employer when they're interviewing for a job. That's really a personal decision. Especially for teens, many believe that telling others they're GLBTQ should be on a "need to know" basis, unless it somehow relates to the job.

Some people who are completely out prefer to be open about who they are from the very beginning to make sure their gender identity or sexual orientation won't be a problem in the workplace. But telling an employer that you're GLBTQ during an interview can create an uncomfortable situation for you both. Whether you're GLBTQ or straight doesn't have anything to do with how you do your job, but coming out in the interview might give that impression. The focus is really on finding out whether the job is a good match for you and whether the company is GLBTQ-friendly. You don't have to come out to do that.

Here are questions you can ask to determine whether a company is queer-friendly:

1. Ask about the company's policies.

"Do you have an employment nondiscrimination policy? Who does it cover?" or "Does your employment nondiscrimination policy cover GLBTQ people?"

2. You can ask "How is this workplace environment for GLBTQ employees?"

This gives an obvious indication that you're GLBTQ, so it's up to you to decide if you're comfortable with that.

Some people who are transgender choose to come out during an interview especially if they dress as the opposite anatomical sex. Unfortunately, workplace discrimination against transgender people is still largely accepted. (The companies on page 189 that scored 100 percent on the HRC *Corporate Equality Index* all include gender identity in their nondiscrimination policies.) Groups like HRC, GenderPAC, and the National Transgender Advocacy Association are fighting to have policy makers include "gender identity" in the employment nondiscrimination legislation.

Should I Come Out to My Coworkers?

Coming out to coworkers can be a great experience because it can result in a more open and supportive work environment, one where you feel free to be yourself. But remember, people who you work with don't have to be your best friends; it's up to you how much personal information you want them to know.

As you spend more time in the working world, you'll come across people whose personal opinions—religious, political, social—are very different from yours. Sometimes these encounters can be stressful or annoying. But, for some of the people you're exposed to, you may be the first queer person they've ever knowingly met and just knowing you could be a very positive experience for them.

For those who prefer not to come out as GLBTQ at work, that's okay. It's important to do what you're comfortable with.

What Are My Rights?

Presently, there isn't a federal antidiscrimination law that protects GLBTQ people from job discrimination, so queer rights in the workplace vary by employer and geographic location. Some states have enacted antidiscrimination laws that cover job discrimination, and many include housing and public accommodations as well. (Unfortunately, some states have passed more hostile legislation like laws banning same-sex marriages.) So, at least for now, your rights depend on where you live or work.

BEEN THERE

"I think that the quality of life for GLBTQ people in this country is getting better, but it certainly isn't great. There are a lot of benefits and rights that GLBTQ people are not allowed to receive. Being gay didn't really affect me negatively until I started to witness the hatred and bigotry in this world. But once I started to get out and see that other gay people have made it through, I started to feel much better about being a gay person in this country."—Robert, 15

More progressive companies have added phrases like "sexual orientation" and "gender identity" to their nondiscrimination policies, so while their home state may not have protections in place for queer people, the company does.

Civil rights and GLBTQ activists are currently lobbying hard to get the Employment Non-Discrimination Act (ENDA) passed. If passed, ENDA would be a federal law that provides basic protections against discrimination in the workplace because of sexual orientation. (It currently doesn't include gender identity.) It would make it illegal to fire, deny employment, or harass someone because of his or her actual or perceived sexual orientation. Many major corporations including Microsoft and Nike have endorsed this bill.

Find Out More About the Law

To learn more about ENDA and the most current information about laws where you live, visit HRC's Issues page at *www.hrc.org*. You can also call HRC at (202) 628-4160. Additionally, Lambda Legal has similar information at their Web site at *www.lambdalegal.org*. Also check out the Web site for the Equal Employment Opportunity Commission (EEOC) at *www.eeoc.gov* for information on state and federal employment laws.

I Am Being Discriminated Against in My Workplace. What Should I Do?

Discrimination can take many forms. Sexual harassment, off-color remarks, and passing up someone for a promotion because he is GLBTQ are all forms of discrimination. Queer people do sometimes face workplace discrimination, but you should neither expect it or accept it.

Here are some tips for what to do if you think you are being discriminated against by an employer:

1. Stop and think.

Think carefully about the situation. Are you sure you're being discriminated against because you're GLBTQ? You might be. It's also possible that you're misreading the situation. Stop and assess it. Does your employer have a history of anti-GLBTQ behavior? Could you have misunderstood something that was said?

2. Write it down.

If you suspect you're being discriminated against because you're GLBTQ, write down the incident and include names of anyone else who might have witnessed it. If there are several incidents, keep track of all of them. Keep a record of any interactions you have with your employer regarding the matter and include her responses. This record will be very useful if the issue is not resolved and you decide to take further action.

3. Come up with a plan.

Plan what you will say to your employer and approach her calmly and rationally. If you march into her office with accusations, chances are she will react negatively. Ask to speak with her and then sit down and explain the situation and why you feel you were discriminated against.

Then listen to her response. She might offer an explanation that puts your concerns to rest, she might confess to the discrimination, or she might deny it completely. Regardless of her response, try to stay calm.

4. If her response is negative, decide your course of action.

You have several options. You can go back to work and ignore it, you can quit your job, or you can try to address the issue. There isn't one right way to deal with the situation, just what's right for you. You might not have the time, energy, or money (in the case of a legal response) to address the issue. You might really need the job. Or you might feel like the situation is one you just can't live with.

If you decide to pursue the matter, HRC and Lambda Legal are two groups that can counsel you about your rights according to your state's laws. They can also refer you to lawyers in your area, if necessary.

Discrimination can be demeaning and frustrating. Regardless of how you decide to deal with it, be sure to remind yourself that discrimination is a result of ignorance, and it has nothing to do with you as a person.

A Perfect Match:
Finding the Right School

If you're going to college, picking the right college (or technical or vocational school) can be challenging. First you have to go through what every other college-bound teen goes through: deciding on a state school or a private college; choosing a liberal arts program or something more specialized; figuring out what you can afford; applying for scholarships or financial aid. But once you've narrowed it down, how can you be sure you will be going into an environment that's supportive of GLBTQ people?

Tips for Finding a GLBTQ-Friendly College

If you are interested in finding a GLBTQ-friendly college, it's not as hard as you might think. Here's some information and ideas that may help make your search a little easier:

Search the Internet.

Using a search engine, you can look for schools using terms like "gay-friendly colleges." Many queer Web sites and publications often run articles about queer-friendly colleges. Some of them even poll their readers to find out what's what.

You can also use the Web to take a closer look at colleges that you're interested in. You may be able to find out a lot of information before you ever consider going for a visit. You can look up their nondiscrimination policy, peruse majors and course listings, find out about student groups, and even learn more about the city or area where the college is located.

Check out a "best colleges" guide.

There are several "best colleges" guides available. One of the most well-known is the *U.S. News and World Report College Guide.* Another guide series, *Best 345 Colleges* by the Princeton Review, includes a listing of the colleges that are most accepting of the queer community. The list includes the top queer-friendly colleges as well as the most queer-friendly geographic areas for college students.

These are the top twenty schools listed in the 2003 edition of the *Best 345 Colleges* where the "gay community" is accepted:

1. Drew University (New Jersey)
2. Boston University
3. Wesleyan University (Connecticut)
4. Wellesley College (Massachusetts)
5. Vassar College (New York)
6. Smith College (Massachusetts)
7. Sarah Lawrence College (New York)
8. Colby College (Maine)
9. New York University
10. University of California at Santa Cruz
11. Grinnell College (Iowa)
12. Mount Holyoke College (Massachusetts)
13. Harvey Mudd College (California)
14. Worcester Polytechnic Institute (Massachusetts)
15. Macalester College (Minnesota)
16. Wells College (New York)
17. Brandeis University (Massachusetts)
18. University of California at Berkeley
19. Stanford University (California)
20. Dickinson College (Pennsylvania)

The list is a result of a survey of 100,000 students that asks 70 questions on topics from academics and the school's administration to the quality of student life. Included among the questions is "Students, faculty, and administrators treat all persons equally regardless of their sexual orientation," and those surveyed are asked to respond based on a scale that ranges from "agree strongly" to "disagree strongly."

The schools on the list certainly aren't the only queer-friendly schools in the country (or the world for that matter, if you're thinking internationally). But if picking a queer-friendly school is one of your primary concerns, such lists are a good place to start.

Investigate your colleges of choice.

What if you have your heart set on a school that's not on one of these lists? Or you've found a school that you're really curious about? Just because a school hasn't earned an official queer-friendly designation, doesn't mean that it's not. It helps to keep an open mind, because you may find that your perfect school is one that you'd never even heard of when you first started looking. Here are some ways to find out if the schools you're interested in are queer-friendly:

- **Get a copy of the school's nondiscrimination policy.** All colleges have one. Look in the student handbook or an admissions guidebook. It might even be posted at their Web site. If you see "sexual orientation" and hopefully "gender identity" as categories protected from discrimination, that's a good sign. If those words aren't there, you might not have any recourse if you become a victim of harassment or discrimination by the college or by other students at the college.

> **BEEN THERE**
> "I've come out to my closest friends from home, but I'm out to my whole campus now, being the GSA's copresident this year. As a college freshman, I was re-closeted. I didn't have anyone to talk to and just felt lost. I finally found the on-campus Alliance and have been active ever since."—Elena, 20

- **Investigate the campus climate.** Does the campus have a GLBTQ student group? Is it active? Some campuses even have GLBTQ resource or community centers.

RESOURCE

GLBTQ Campus Directory

To find a listing of schools with GLBTQ resource and community centers, visit the Web site of the National Consortium of Directors of Lesbian, Gay, Bisexual, and Transgender Resources in Higher Education at *www.lgbtcampus.org.*

▪ **Talk to students.** If there is a GLBTQ group or GSA on campus, you can contact them and talk with one or more of the students. Most of these groups are happy to help.

▪ **Check out the curriculum.** If a school includes a "queer studies" or similar curriculum, or even a few courses such as "gender studies," "gay and lesbian history," or "sexuality and gender in anthropology," chances are it's a pretty friendly place, at least academically. Although entire queer studies programs or majors aren't commonplace yet, many schools have at least one or more offerings on topics like queer theory or gender in society. Departments like English, Literature, Political Science, Sociology, and Theatre are also frequently home to courses on queer topics. A lot of the class information should be available online, or you can call the school and ask to speak with someone in a particular department or in an academic administrator's office.

It helps to remember that the right college for you is made up of many factors, not the least of which is academics. If a college doesn't have the courses you're interested in or the major you want, it's not going to be a great match for you even if it does appear to be queer-friendly or have an "official" queer-friendly designation.

Check out the surrounding area.

When you leave for college, unless you're sticking close to home, you're also moving to another community. You'll want to do some investigating into that area to find out if it's GLBTQ-friendly. You don't have to go to school in a city to be in a queer-friendly area. Many schools in suburban and rural areas are friendly.

Visit the schools you're most interested in.

If you can, visit the schools you're most interested in attending. You can learn a lot on a campus visit that guide books, college materials, and guidance counselors don't cover. This may be a good time to explore the GLBTQ resource or community center or meet people in the school's GLBTQ group. Even if you can't do that, simple things like eating in a dining hall, reading the flyers on campus bulletin boards, and looking through the campus newspaper can tell you a lot about a school's culture and quality of life. Pay attention to how you feel being on campus. Do you feel comfortable or are certain things making you nervous? This is all information you can use when it comes time to decide where you're going to college.

Fraternities and Sororities

Have a dream of being in a sorority or fraternity? Lots of GLBTQ people are members of a sorority or fraternity. In fact, Delta Lambda Phi is a fraternity that bills itself as being "for gay, bisexual, and progressive men." For more information on Delta Lambda Phi, visit their Web site at *www.dlp.org* or call 1-800-558-2295. There are other Greek organizations that bill themselves as queer-friendly, although some of this depends on the particular campus more than the parent organization. The Lambda 10 Project is an organization for GLBTQ Greeks and addresses a variety of issues that can be part of being Greek and queer. Its Web site *(www.lambda10.org)* also features news and resources and hosts a bulletin board for GLBTQ Greeks. The point is, if you dream of being a sorority chick or a frat daddy, you don't have to give that up because you're queer.

Note: ♂ is the international symbol for male. ♀ is the international symbol for female. ⚧ is a common symbol used to represent transgender.

Going with the Flow:
Some Thoughts on Growing Up

Leaving high school is a big transition for all teens. For GLBTQ teens it can be the gateway to a whole new world. With increased independence, you'll most likely have greater access to other GLBTQ people, especially if you move to an urban area. You may discover a completely different social world, which can be exhilarating, scary, and a big relief. You'll finally have more control over your environment than you did when you were in high school.

You may find that all of the experiences you had up through high school—even the really difficult ones—helped make you a pretty strong and amazing person.

All of this change and transition makes for an exciting time. It can be tempting to do everything you weren't able to do before like spend most of your time socializing, dating, and going out. With the sudden increase in access to a whole new community, it can be easy to get carried away. The same instincts that helped you take care of yourself and keep it together until graduation are still valuable to you.

Trust yourself to make the decisions that are best for you. Even though the scenery and the people may have changed, your instincts haven't. So, explore and discover new ideas and people, and most of all, enjoy yourself and your life. You deserve it.

BEEN THERE

"The best thing about being GLBTQ is that there is so much diversity in the community. There is so much more than being GLBTQ that makes us who we are, it's just one thing that brings us together. We know how not to be judgmental of others and we grow together. When one person in this community does something positive it affects everyone, and that is important. We always move one step forward, together."—Elena, 20

GLOSSARY

A word about words. Some people are offended by the use of words like "queer," "dyke," and "fag" because they once had extremely negative connotations and were primarily used as insults. These words have been reclaimed or "taken back" by many in the GLBTQ community. Now, GLBTQ people use words like queer, dyke, and fag as a means of asserting pride in who they are.

As you read this glossary, keep in mind that the language of the GLBTQ community is always changing. Words aren't always perfect, or even as exact as we would like them to be, but without them we wouldn't be able to talk about GLBTQ issues. And talking about queerness is one of the most important things we can do.

anatomy: The physical characteristics of the body, often used in reference to a specific sex. An anatomical male has a penis and testicles. An anatomical female has a vagina, a vulva, ovaries, a clitoris, and breasts. People whose anatomy doesn't match their gender identity are called transgender.

androgynes/gender benders/ gender blenders: People who are androgynous or who are gender benders/blenders merge what are stereotypically male and female characteristics in many different ways. Some are subtle and some are considered shocking. Someone who is androgynous may not be obviously male or female at first glance (or even second or third glance). There are also people who blend genders, for example, "riot grrls" might shave their heads and wear combat boots, but also wear makeup and a skirt. Some famous examples of gender benders are k.d. lang, Annie Lennox, David Bowie, Boy George, and Eddie Izzard. Being androgynous or a gender bender is not necessarily a reflection of sexual orientation or gender identity.

asexual: A lack of sexual feelings toward men or women.

bisexual: A person who is emotionally, romantically, and sexually attracted to people of either sex.

biological sex: The sex someone is born as. Also referred to as birth sex, anatomical sex, physical sex.

butch: A term used to describe both males and females who act and dress in stereotypically masculine ways.

closeted: A person who does not disclose his or her sexual orientation or gender identity. People may also be partially closeted— only coming out to a select few.

coming out: Disclosing one's sexual orientation or gender identity to others. Some people never come out, some come out to a few individuals, others come out to many people at once, and for others the coming out process takes place more slowly.

crossdressers: Crossdressers are people who dress in the clothing of the opposite sex. They may do this in private or try to pass as the opposite sex in public. Crossdressers used to be called transvestites. They can be male

or female and can be straight, gay, lesbian, or bisexual.

drag queens/drag kings: Drag queens (men who dress as women) and drag kings (women who dress as men) usually present larger than life representations of men and women. They exaggerate stereotypes of men and women, usually for entertainment (think RuPaul). Dressing as a drag queen or king is not necessarily a reflection of sexual orientation or gender identity. Drag queens or kings can be GLBTQ or straight, they may be crossdressers, or they may just dress as the opposite sex when they are entertaining.

femme: A term used to describe both males and females who act and dress in stereotypically feminine ways.

FTM, also F-T-M and F2M: Stands for female-to-male. Refers to transgender people who were born with female bodies but who have a predominantly male gender identity. They may express this with their appearance (clothes, hair, etc.) or they may opt for a physical change that can involve hormones and/or surgery.

gay: This term is often used to describe both homosexual men and homosexual women, though it is more commonly used to refer to homosexual men. As it refers to men, gay describes men who are emotionally, romantically, and sexually attracted to other men. The word "gay" didn't come into wide use to describe homosexual people until the 1950s. Before that, it was used as a code word for same-sex sexuality.

Gay-Straight Alliance (GSA): A student club for gay, lesbian, bisexual, transgender, and questioning students as well as their straight allies. GSAs can provide a social haven and support for queer students. They can also work for positive change on GLBTQ issues within a school or school system. GSAs are legally entitled to exist according to a federal court ruling.

gender: While this word may be used to describe anatomy, it's really about a person's identity as feminine or masculine rather than the physical characteristics that make someone female or male. Gender is made up of many things, including behaviors, cultural traits, and psychological traits that are associated with a specific sex.

gender dysphoria: A term for the pain, anxiety, and confusion that can result when there is a disparity between a person's gender identity and biological sex. Pressure to conform to accepted gender roles and expression, and a general lack of acceptance from society also contribute to it.

gender expression: How you express your gender identity. It includes your clothes, your hairstyle, your body language (how you walk, your posture, your gestures, your mannerisms), and even your speech patterns. In society, people often take their cues from someone's gender expression to decide that person's anatomical sex.

gender identity: Your internal sense of being male or female—it's whether you consider or feel yourself to be male or female. A person's gender identity doesn't necessarily reflect her or his biological sex. There are gender activists, like Kate Bornstein, who believe it's possible to have a gender identity that's male, female, or something else entirely.

gender identity disorder (GID): Mental health professionals often diagnose transgender people with GID. A diagnosis of GID lets transgender people get mental and physical treatment, which can be especially helpful for people trying to physically transition their gender, but a diagnosis of GID can also carry the stigma of mental illness.

gender transitioning: Gender transitioning is a complex, multi-step process of starting to live in a way that accurately reflects a transgender person's true gender identity. Transitioning primarily involves social issues such as changing your name, dressing differently, altering other aspects of your appearance like hair or makeup, and changing your mannerisms, voice, and how you move. Transitioning doesn't, by definition, include surgery or other physical changes though it may depending on the person. A physical transition may include taking hormones or other substances, under the supervision of a medical professional. For some, transitioning may also include surgery.

GLBTQ: An acronym that stands for gay, lesbian, bisexual, transgender, and questioning.

heterosexism: The idea that heterosexual people are the norm and that GLBTQ people are somehow abnormal; the assumption that people are heterosexual. Heterosexism contributes to homophobia.

heterosexual: People who are emotionally and physically attracted to people of the opposite sex.

homophobia: Homophobia is when someone feels a negative emotion like fear, anger, or suspicion toward someone else for being GLBTQ. Homophobia can also take the form of ignorance about GLBTQ people. Homophobia can be very overt, like someone shouting "dyke!" or "fag!" in the hall, or it can be more subtle, like a teammate quietly trying to avoid being near you in the locker room.

homosexual: People who are emotionally and physically attracted to people of the same sex.

intersex: People who are born with a mixture of both male and female genitals or with ambiguous genitalia. In many cases, the doctor or the parents "choose" their child's anatomy and the child has a series of surgeries throughout infancy and childhood to definitively assign one anatomical sex. The surgery doesn't always result in a physical sex assignment that matches the person's internal gender. As a result, some intersex people grow up having gender identity issues that mirror those experienced by transgender people.

lesbian: A woman who is emotionally, romantically, and sexually attracted to other women.

MTF, also M-T-F, M2F: Stands for male-to-female. Refers to people who were born with male bodies but who have a predominantly female gender identity. They may express this with their appearance (clothes, hair, etc.) or they may opt for a physical change that can involve the use of hormones and possibly surgery.

out: Living openly as a queer person. When GLBTQ people tell other people that they are queer, the process is called "coming out," as in "coming out of the closet." Being outed is when someone accidentally or purposefully reveals another person's sexual orientation or gender identity, often before that person is ready or can do so.

passing: Being able to be accepted in society as someone of a different biological sex. Being able to pass is important for transgender people, especially those who want to completely transition physically. They have to undergo a real-life test where they live as their correct gender identity for a period of time before surgery is performed.

queer: Refers to GLBTQ people. Sometimes used as a slur, the term has been reclaimed by many GLBTQ people who use it as an expression of pride. Some GLBTQ people prefer to identify as queer rather than gay, lesbian, bisexual, or transgender, because they feel it encompasses more of who they are or gives a greater sense of unity with the entire community.

questioning: Being uncertain of one's sexual orientation or gender identity.

sexual behavior: Sexual behavior only describes sexual activity, not sexual identity. For example, a man may identify as gay but still engage in sexual behavior with women. That's still considered heterosexual behavior. Or a woman may not identify as a lesbian but she may take part in sexual activity with a woman. That is homosexual behavior.

sexual identity: How a person views and identifies himself or herself in terms of his or her sexual orientation or behavior. Some people may identify as gay, lesbian, bisexual, or straight; other people may refuse to identify with a particular label. Some GLBTQ people choose to identify as queer for this reason. An individual's sexual identity is decided by that person, so a person who participates in straight sexual behavior may still identify as gay, lesbian, or bisexual and vice versa. A person's sexual identity can change over the course of his or her life.

sexual orientation: A term used to describe who someone is emotionally, romantically, and sexually attracted to. Gay, lesbian, bisexual, and straight all describe different forms of sexual orientation. Sexual orientation—and being queer—isn't just about who you have sex with. Because of that there have been suggestions for a more accurate phrase, such as "emotional orientation" or "affectional orientation." But for now, sexual orientation is the common phrase.

sex reassignment surgery (SRS): In sex reassignment surgery, a surgeon modifies the primary sex characteristics (the genitals). Some transsexuals who need a complete physical transformation undergo SRS in conjunction with hormone therapy. It is sometimes accompanied by surgeries on secondary sex characteristics as well (breasts, Adam's apple) or cosmetic surgery.

straight: Synonymous with heterosexual.

transgender: When you're transgender, you have a gender identity or gender expression that is different from your biological sex or physical anatomy. A few definitions may be helpful here. Transgender is a broad term that covers many groups. It can include transsexuals (in all stages), crossdressers, drag kings and queens, and people who are intersex, among many others. People who are trans

206 GLBTQ: The Survival Guide for Queer & Questioning Teens

may identify themselves in a variety of ways. Being transgender isn't a reflection of sexual orientation. Transgender people are often straight, but they can also be gay, lesbian, or bisexual.

transitioning: See *gender transitioning.*

transphobia: Transphobia is when someone feels a negative emotion like fear, anger, or suspicion toward someone else for being transgender. Transphobia can also take the form of ignorance about transgender people.

transsexual: Often used interchangeably with "transgender," though there has been some controversy over this. Generally it refers to people who don't identify with the sex they were born and who may change their bodies through hormones and possibly surgery to reconcile their gender identity and physical sex. All transsexuals are transgender, but not all transgender people are transsexuals.

Two Spirit: Certain Native American cultures described transgender people as having "two spirits." Generally Two-Spirited people were born into one sex but took on the gender roles for both sexes (though this definition varies somewhat across cultures). Today, some transgender people identify as "Two Spirit."

RESOURCES

It's nearly impossible to create an exhaustive list of all of the GLBTQ resources because there are so many. This information is intended to give you an idea of what's available and to provide you with starting points to explore a variety of topics.

Additional resources, as well as more detailed explanations of many of the resources listed here, can be found in the text. The Selected Bibliography on pages 213–215 also includes some materials that may be of interest.

Books and Publications

Always My Child: A Parent's Guide to Understanding Your Gay, Lesbian, Bisexual, Transgendered or Questioning Son or Daughter by Kevin Jennings with Pat Shapiro, M.S.W. (New York: Fireside/Simon & Schuster Inc., 2003). A friendly, thorough, and practical guide that helps put the pieces together for parents or guardians trying to understand their queer or questioning child. By the executive director of GLSEN.

The Celluloid Closet: Homosexuality in the Movies by Vito Russo (New York: Harper & Row, 1987). A groundbreaking study of how queer people have been depicted in the movies since film making began.

Changing Bodies, Changing Lives: A Book for Teens on Sex and Relationships by Ruth Bell and the Teen Book Project (New York: Three Rivers Press, 1998). Thorough and nonjudgmental information on sexuality and a wide range of emotional and physical issues affecting teens, including general emotional and physical health care, sexual harassment and violence, and sexually transmitted infections.

A Desired Past: A Short History of Same-Sex Love in America by Leila J. Rupp (Chicago: University of Chicago Press, 2002). A broad introductory history that covers 400 years of American same-sex love and relationships.

Free Your Mind: The Book for Gay, Lesbian, and Bisexual Youth—and Their Allies by Ellen Bass and Kate Kaufman (New York: HarperPerennial, 1996). A comprehensive resource with information and practical advice for GLBTQ youth and their allies.

Gender Outlaw: On Men, Women, and the Rest of Us by Kate Bornstein (New York: Vintage Books, 1995). An entertaining and thought-provoking discussion of what gender is and what it means to be differently gendered.

Hidden from History: Reclaiming the Gay & Lesbian Past edited by Martin Duberman, Martha Vicinus, and George Chauncey Jr. (New York: New American Library, 1989). A collection of 30 essays exploring same-sex relationships in different cultures and eras. Essay topics include women who passed as men in 19th century America, "mine marriages" in South African gold mines, and lesbian sexuality in certain Native American cultures.

Our Trans Children by Jessica Xavier, Courtney Sharp, and Mary Boenke (Washington, DC: Parents, Families and Friends of Lesbians and Gays, 2001). An extremely helpful booklet full of detailed information for anyone who wants to know more about being transgender.

Stonewall by Martin Duberman (New York: Plume, 1994). A history of the Stonewall uprising, the people involved in it, and the early years of the Gay Liberation Movement.

Surpassing the Love of Men: Romantic Friendship and Love Between Women from the Renaissance to the Present by Lillian Faderman (New York: Quill, 2001). A reissue of the classic history of 500 years of love, desire, and relationships between women.

Two Teenagers in Twenty: Writings by Gay and Lesbian Youth edited by Ann Heron (Los Angeles: Alyson Publications, 1995). First-person accounts by gay and lesbian teens about discovering one's sexual orientation, coming out to family and friends, and the effects—positive, negative, and mixed—of these realizations and actions.

When Nothing Matters Anymore: A Survival Guide for Depressed Teens by Bev Cobain, R.N.,C. (Minneapolis: Free Spirit Publishing, 2007). A book for teens on how to recognize depression, get help, and stay well. Full of survival tips, resources, and stories from teens—including some GLBTQ teens.

Organizations

American Civil Liberties Union (ACLU)
125 Broad Street, 18th Floor
New York, NY 10004
www.aclu.org
The ACLU works in the courts to defend civil liberties for all people. It has a Lesbian and Gay Rights section, which includes transgender issues, queer students in schools, and domestic partnerships.

Gay & Lesbian Alliance Against Defamation (GLAAD)
104 West 29th Street, 4th Floor
New York, NY 10001
(212) 629-3322
www.glaad.org
GLAAD works to promote and ensure fair, accurate, and inclusive representation of GLBTQ people and events in all forms of media, from newspapers to movies. Their Web site includes articles and resources related to their work.

Gay and Lesbian Medical Association (GLMA)
459 Fulton Street, Suite 107
San Francisco, CA 94102
(415) 255-4547
www.glma.org
An organization of gay and lesbian medical professionals. It provides referrals to local queer-friendly medical professionals.

Gay, Lesbian and Straight Education Network (GLSEN)
121 West 27th Street, Suite 804
New York, NY 10001
(212) 727-0135
www.glsen.org
glsen@glsen.org
GLSEN works to create safe schools for all GLBTQ people but especially students. They offer a variety of resources and information, much of which is available at their Web site, including: instructions for starting a gay-straight

alliance, information about their "Safe Schools Action Network," an expansive resource center, true stories from GLBTQ teens, and a district locator for information and GSAs in your area.

Gender Education and Advocacy (GEA)
P.O. Box 65
Kensington, MD 20895
www.gender.org
GEA works to provide gender education and advocates for the transgender community. Their Web site includes a wide array of resources including health and employment information, links, news, and a library of trans information.

Gender Public Advocacy Coalition (GenderPAC)
1731 Connecticut Avenue NW, 4th Floor
Washington, DC 20009
(202) 462-6610
www.gpac.org
gpac@gpac.org
GenderPAC is a group that works to fight discrimination and violence that results from gender stereotypes. Their Web site includes information on job discrimination, hate crimes, their youth outreach program, and legislative initiatives.

Hetrick Martin Institute
2 Astor Place
New York, NY 10003
(212) 674-2400
www.hmi.org
info@hmi.org
Hetrick Martin provides direct services and referrals for GLBTQ people ages 12 to 21. Their Web site includes good information and links to other resources.

Human Rights Campaign (HRC)
1640 Rhode Island Avenue NW
Washington, DC 20036
(202) 628-4160
www.hrc.org
HRC works to protect the rights of and improve the quality of life for GLBTQ

people. Their Web site includes a vast amount of information and resources on topics such as National Coming Out Day, workplace issues, and news and legislative updates.

International Foundation for Gender Education (IFGE)
P.O. Box 540229
Waltham, MA 02454
(781) 899-2212
www.ifge.org
IFGE is a transgender advocacy and educational organization. It maintains a bookstore and publishes a magazine on transgender issues. It also provides telephone referrals. The Web site has a wide variety of links and information.

Intersex Society of North America
979 Golf Course Drive, Suite 282
Rohnert Park, CA 94928
www.isna.org
A public awareness, education, and advocacy organization for intersex people, their Web site has news and detailed information (also in Spanish), including an FAQ, an intersex library, and a variety of resources and links.

Lambda Legal Defense and Education Fund
120 Wall Street, Suite 1500
New York, NY 10005
(212) 809-8585
www.lambdalegal.org
legalhelpdesk@lambdalegal.org
Lambda Legal works to protect the civil rights of GLBTQ people. Their Web site includes a variety of resources including a state-by-state directory of legislation concerning queer people and a directory of their regional offices. Also includes resources and information in Spanish.

National Center for Transgender Equality (NCTE)
1325 Massachusetts Avenue, Suite 700
Washington, DC 20005
(202) 903-0112
www.nctequality.org
NCTE is a social justice organization dedicated to promoting the equal rights of transgendered people through advocacy and empowerment.

National Gay and Lesbian Task Force (NGLTF)
1325 Massachusetts Avenue NW,
Suite 600
Washington, DC 20005
(202) 393-5177
www.thetaskforce.org
NGLTF works to fight prejudice and violence against GLBTQ people at the local, state, and national levels. Among the many services they provide are legal assistance and referrals to attorneys, doctors, counselors, and other professionals; a publications library; and academic scholarships and internships for GLBTQ journalism students. Visit their Web site for information about these services and more.

National Transgender Advocacy Coalition (NTAC)
P.O. Box 76027
Washington, DC 20013
www.ntac.org
NTAC is an education and advocacy organization that works to attain full civil rights for transgender and intersex people and combats discrimination through legal means and activism.

National Youth Advocacy Coalition (NYAC)
1638 R Street NW, Suite 300
Washington, DC 20009
1-800-541-6922
www.nyacyouth.org
NYAC is a group that works to improve the lives of GLBTQ youth. Their Web site includes a National Resources

Clearinghouse on GLBTQ youth issues; "Crossroads Magazine," a publication by and for GLBTQ youth and their allies; and information on education, religion, policy, gender identity, youth of color, and other issues.

OutProud: The National Coalition for Gay, Lesbian, Bisexual, and Transgender Youth
369 Third Street, Suite B-362
San Rafael, CA 94901
www.outproud.org
info@outproud.org
OutProud's information-packed Web site includes news, coming out stories, links to local resources, discussion groups, online brochures, a school resources library, and a community role models archive.

Parents, Families and Friends of Lesbians and Gays (PFLAG)
1726 M Street NW, Suite 400
Washington, DC 20036
(202) 467-8180
www.pflag.org
info@pflag.org
PFLAG provides materials and support services not only for friends and family, but also for GLBTQ people themselves. Their Web site includes information about their programs, including their extensive safe schools campaign. The site also includes electronic versions of many of their pamphlets. PFLAG has chapters all over the country and you can find the chapter nearest you by searching the directory at their Web site or by contacting them.

Sexual Minority Youth Assistance League (SMYAL)
410 7th Street SE
Washington, DC 20003
(202) 546–5940
www.smyal.org
SMYAL is a youth service agency devoted to increasing public awareness and understanding of sexual minority

issues. SMYAL supports and strives to enhance the self-esteem of sexual minority youth—anyone ages 13 to 21 who is lesbian, gay, bisexual, transgender, or may be questioning their sexual identity.

Hotlines

CDC Information Hotline
1-800-232-4636
A service of the CDC, this hotline provides anonymous, confidential information on HIV, AIDS, and sexually transmitted infections (STIs) and how to prevent them. It also provides referrals to clinical and other services. Operates 24 hours a day, 7 days a week.

Gay and Lesbian National Hotline
1-888-THE-GLNH (1-888-843-4564)
GLNH is staffed by counselors Monday–Friday, 4PM–12AM, and Saturday, 12PM–5PM (Eastern Standard Time). Staff provides crisis counseling, referrals, lists of shelters, and other information. You can find out more online at *www.glnh.org* or by emailing glnh@glnh.org.

Girls and Boys Town National Hotline
1-800-448-3000
The Girls and Boys Town National Hotline is a crisis hotline for teens that you can call 24 hours a day. Professional counselors listen and offer advice on any issue, including depression, suicide, and identity struggles.

National Hopeline Network
1-800-784-2433
The National Hopeline Network is for people who are depressed or suicidal, or who are concerned about someone else. The line connects callers to the nearest certified and available Crisis Center, where trained counselors answer 24 hours a day, 7 days a week. You should reach a trained counselor in 20 to 30 seconds and never get a busy signal or voicemail.

National Runaway Switchboard Hotline
1-800-786-2929
This is a toll-free, 24-hour hotline that provides confidential crisis intervention for a variety of issues, including depression and suicide, and referrals for teens and their families. They can help connect you with counseling services in your area.

Rape, Abuse and Incest National Network (RAINN) National Sexual Assault Hotline
1-800-656-HOPE (1-800-656-4673)
A hotline run by the largest anti-sexual violence organization in the United States. It provides free, confidential counseling, information, and support.

Trevor Helpline
1-866-4-U-TREVOR (1-866-488-7386)
The Trevor Helpline is a 24-hour, toll-free crisis hotline for GLBTQ youth and teens. They also have a Web site at *www.thetrevorproject.org* with information about how to help someone who is suicidal and support groups and resources for GLBTQ teens.

Web sites

Oasis Magazine

www.oasisjournals.com
Oasis is an online magazine by and for
GLBTQ teens. Articles and columns
cover a wide variety of topics. Also
includes an online member discussion
forum and access to user blogs.

TransProud

www.transproud.org
TransProud is OutProud's Web site for
transgender youth. It has news, information, an FAQ, resources, and dozens
of first-person stories from trans teens.

Youth Guardian Services

www.youth-guard.org
This Web site provides online support
services for GLBT youth and offers free
subscriptions to several informative
email lists.

Youth Resource

www.youthresource.com
A wide-ranging and excellent site for
GLBTQ teens from all different backgrounds. The site combines peer advi-
sors with information, resources, and
first-person stories about a variety of
topics including being disabled and
GLBTQ, staying healthy, being transgender, religion, relationships, and being
GLBTQ and a teen of color.

SELECTED BIBLIOGRAPHY

AIDS Epidemic Update: December 2002 (Geneva, Switzerland: Joint United Nations Programme on HIV/AIDS and World Health Organization, 2002).

"Answers to Your Questions About Sexual Orientation and Homosexuality" (Washington, DC: American Psychological Association, 1998).

"Be Yourself: Questions & Answers for Gay, Lesbian, Bisexual & Transgendered Youth" (Washington, DC: Parents, Families and Friends of Lesbians and Gays, 1999).

Bornstein, Kate. *Gender Outlaw: On Men, Women, and the Rest of Us.* New York: Vintage Books, 1995.

Bozett, Frederick, and Marvin Sussman, editors. *Homosexuality and Family Relations.* Binghamton, NY: Harrington Park Press, 1990.

Carter, Kelley. "Gay Slurs Abound." *The Des Moines Register* (March 7, 1997).

Cobain, Bev. *When Nothing Matters Anymore.* Minneapolis: Free Spirit Publishing, 1998.

Dangerous Liaisons: Substance Abuse and Sex (New York: National Center on Addiction and Substance Abuse at Columbia University, 1999).

Diamant, Allison, et al. "Lesbians' Sexual History with Men: Implications for Taking a Sexual History." *Archives of Internal Medicine* 159: 2730–2736 (1999).

Diamond, Milton, and H. Keith Sigmundson. "Management of Intersexuality: Guidelines for Dealing with Persons with Ambiguous Genitalia." *Archives of Pediatrics and Adolescent Medicine* 151: 1046–1050 (October 1997).

"Domestic Partner Benefits." An online document from the Human Rights Campaign WorkNet *(www.hrc.org/issues/4877.htm).*

"Domestic Violence in Gay, Lesbian, and Bisexual Relationships." An online document from Lambda Gay & Lesbian Anti-Violence Project *(www.lambda.org/DV_background.htm)*

Duberman, Martin, Martha Vicinus, and George Chauncey Jr., editors. *Hidden from History: Reclaiming the Gay & Lesbian Past.* New York: Meridian, 1990.

"Enrollment Status of the Population 3 Years Old and Over, by Age, Sex, Race, Hispanic Origin, Nativity, and Selected Educational Characteristics" (Washington, DC: U.S. Census Bureau, 2000).

"Facts: Gay and Lesbian Youth in Schools" (New York: Lambda Legal Defense and Education Fund, 2002).

"Fact Sheet: Lesbian, Gay, Bisexual and Transgender Youth Issues" (Washington, DC: Sexuality Information and Education Council of the United States, 2001).

"Fact Sheet: Teen Sexual Activity" (Menlo Park, CA: Henry J. Kaiser Family Foundation, August 2000).

Freedner, Naomi, et al. "Dating Violence Among Gay, Lesbian, and Bisexual Adolescents: Results from a Community Survey." *Journal of Adolescent Health* 31(6): 469–474 (2002).

"Gay-Straight Clubs Formed by Public School Students: Why School Officials Need to Treat Them Equally" (New York: American Civil Liberties Union Lesbian and Gay Rights Project, Lambda Legal Defense and Education Fund, and the National Center for Lesbian Rights, 2000).

"Guidelines for Psychotherapy with Lesbian, Gay, and Bisexual Clients" (Washington, DC: American Psychological Association, 2000).

"A Guide to Effective Statewide Laws/Policies: Preventing Discrimination Against LGBT Students in K–12 Schools." A joint publication from Lambda and GLSEN (January 15, 2002).

Hatred in the Hallways: Violence and Discrimination Against Lesbian, Gay, Bisexual, and Transgender Students in U.S. Schools (New York: Human Rights Watch, 2001).

"HIV/AIDS Policy Fact Sheet: The Global HIV/AIDS Epidemic" (Menlo Park, CA: Henry J. Kaiser Family Foundation, July 2002).

"HIV/AIDS Policy Fact Sheet: The HIV/AIDS Epidemic in the United States" (Menlo Park, CA: Henry J. Kaiser Family Foundation, July 2002).

Jennings, Kevin, with Pat Shapiro. *Always My Child: A Parent's Guide to Understanding Your Gay, Lesbian, Bisexual, Transgendered, or Questioning Son or Daughter.* New York: Simon and Schuster, 2003.

"Love Doesn't Have to Hurt Teens." An online document from the American Psychological Association *(www.apa.org/pi/pii/teen).*

"Massachusetts Youth Risk Behavior Survey Results" (Malden, MA: Massachusetts Department of Education, 2000).

Morrow, Kate, and Jenifer Allsworth. "Sexual Risk in Lesbian and Bisexual Women." *Gay & Lesbian Medical Association* 4: 149–165 (2000).

"National School Climate Survey" (Washington, DC: Gay, Lesbian and Straight Education Network, 2001).

"National Survey of Family Growth" (Atlanta: U.S. Centers for Disease Control and Prevention, 1995).

Nichols, Jack. Interview with George Weinberg. *Gay Today* (February 3, 1997).

OutPoud/Oasis Internet Survey of Queer and Questioning Youth: 2000 Survey Results Preview. Found at *www.outproud.org/survey/highlights.html.*

"Partnership Attitude Tracking Study (PATS)" (New York: Partnership for a Drug-Free America, 2002).

Perrotti, Jeff, and Kim Westheimer. *When the Drama Club Is Not Enough: Lessons from the Safe Schools Program for Gay and Lesbian Students.* Boston: Beacon Press, 2001.

"Questions and Answers About Gay-Straight Alliances" (Washington, DC: Gay, Lesbian and Straight Education Network and the American Civil Liberties Union, 2001).

Remafedi, Gary, et al. "Demography of Sexual Orientation in Adolescents." *Pediatrics* 89: 714 (1991).

Rupp, Leila J. *A Desired Past: A Short History of Same-Sex Love in America.* Chicago: University of Chicago Press, 1999.

Ryan, Caitlin, and Donna Futterman. *Lesbian & Gay Youth: Care & Counseling.* New York: Columbia University Press, 1998.

Safren, Steven, and Richard Heimberg. "Depression, Hopelessness, Suicidality, and Related Factors in Sexual Minority and Heterosexual Adolescents." *Journal of Consulting and Clinical Psychology* 67(6): 859–866 (1999).

Sathrum, Paul. "When Kids Don't Have a Straight Answer." An online document from the National Education Association *(www.nea.org/neatoday/0103/health.html).*

Savin-Williams, Ritch C. *Mom, Dad. I'm Gay: How Families Negotiate Coming Out.* Washington, DC: American Psychological Association, 2001.

Slezak, Michael. "Drugs." An online document from GayHealth.com *(www.gayhealth.com/iowa-robot/drugs?record=145).*

Standards of Care (Version Six) (Minneapolis: Harry Benjamin International Gender Dysphoria Association, 2001).

"Teen Sex Down New Study Shows" (Atlanta: U.S. Centers for Disease Control and Prevention, May 1997).

"Ten Steps Towards Starting a Gay-Straight Alliance." An online document from the Gay, Lesbian and Straight Education Network *(www.glsen.org).*

"Tracking the Hidden Epidemics: Trends in STDs in the United States" (Atlanta: U.S. Centers for Disease Control and Prevention, 2000).

Troiden, Richard. "The Formation of Homosexual Identities." *Journal of Homosexuality* 17: 43–73 (1989).

"Vermont Youth Risk Behavior Survey" (Burlington, VT: Vermont Department of Health, 2001).

"Washington Transgender Needs Assessment Survey" (Washington, DC: Administration for HIV and AIDS, 2000).

Xavier, Jessica, Courtney Sharp, and Mary Boenke. *Our Trans Children: A Publication of the Transgender Special Outreach Network of Parents, Families, and Friends of Lesbians and Gays (Third Edition).* Washington, DC: Parents, Families and Friends of Lesbians and Gays—Transgender Network, 2001).

Yang, Alan. "From Wrongs to Rights: Public Opinion on Gay and Lesbian Americans Moves Toward Equality." Washington, DC: National Gay and Lesbian Task Force, 1998.

Youth Resource. Quotes appearing in Chapter 8 from Ben, Blake, and Sam are from Youth Resource's Web site *(www.youthresource.com).*

"Youth Risk Behavior Survey" (Atlanta: U.S. Centers for Disease Control and Prevention, 1999).

INDEX

216

ABOUT
THE AUTHOR

Kelly Huegel is a writer and communications professional who has published two books and more than 75 articles. She received critical acclaim for her first book, *Young People and Chronic Illness: True Stories, Help, and Hope*, also published by Free Spirit.

Kelly lives in the Washington, D.C., area and enjoys playing tennis, reading, cooking, and traveling. She also studies martial arts and is a black belt in tae kwon do under Grandmaster Thomas Thompson.

Other Great Books from Free Spirit

More Than a Label
Why What You Wear or Who You're With
Doesn't Define Who You Are
by Aisha Muharrar
Written by a teen, this book empowers students to stand up for themselves, understand others, and consider how labels define, limit, stereotype, and hurt. The book goes beyond labels to consider related issues—including cliques, peer pressure, popularity, racism, self-esteem, sexism, and homophobia. An in-depth look at a topic students can relate to—and for adults, an enlightening journey into the world of teens today. For ages 13 & up.
$13.95; 152 pp.; softcover; B&W photos; 6" x 9"

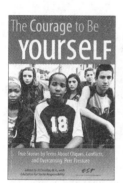

The Courage to Be Yourself
True Stories by Teens About Cliques, Conflicts, and Overcoming Peer Pressure
edited by Al Desetta, with Educators for Social Responsibility
In 26 searingly honest first-person stories, teens tell how they faced the conflicts in their lives and found the courage to be themselves. The Leader's Guide includes activities, exercises, discussions, and reproducibles. For ages 13 & up.
$13.95; 160 pp.; softcover; 6" x 9"

What Do You Really Want?
How to Set a Goal and Go for It! A Guide for Teens
by Beverly K. Bachel
with a special note from polar explorer Ann Bancroft
This book is a step-by-step guide to goal setting, written especially for teens. Each chapter includes fun, creative exercises, practical tips, words of wisdom from famous "goal-getters," real-life examples from teens, and success stories. Includes reproducibles. For ages 11 & up.
$12.95; 144 pp.; softcover; illust.; 6" x 9"

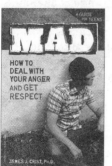

MAD
How to Deal with Your Anger and Get Respect
by James J. Crist, Ph.D.
This practical, supportive book helps teens understand and handle anger. They learn whether they have an anger problem, why we get angry, and how anger affects our bodies and relationships. Practical tools and strategies help them control their anger and avoid poor decisions and actions; insights from real teens let them know they're not alone. The final chapters explore mental health problems that can complicate anger management. Includes resources.
$13.95; 160 pp.; softcover; 2-color; illust.; 6" x 9"

When Nothing Matters Anymore (Revised and Updated)

A Survival Guide for Depressed Teens

by Bev Cobain, R.N.,C.

Personal stories from teens speak directly to readers' feelings, concerns, and experiences. Teens learn how to take care of themselves and how treatment can help. The revised and updated edition includes the latest information on medication, nutrition, and health; current resources; and a Q&A with questions teens have asked over the years. *$14.95; 176 pp.; softcover; 2-color; illust.; 6" x 9"*

The Power to Prevent Suicide (Updated Edition)

A Guide for Teens Helping Teens

by Richard E. Nelson, Ph.D., and Judith C. Galas, new foreword by Bev Cobain, R.N.,C.

When teens consider suicide, they often tell other teens—if not always directly, then in other ways. Updated with new facts, statistics, and resources, this book gives teens the information and insight they need to recognize the risk and respond appropriately. It spells out the warning signs, guides teens through the steps of reaching out to a friend, and explains when and how to seek help. Ages 11 & up. *$13.95; 128 pp.; softcover; 6" x 9"*

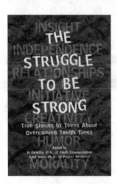

The Struggle to Be Strong

True Stories by Teens About Overcoming Tough Times

edited by Al Desetta, M.A., of Youth Communication, and Sybil Wolin, Ph.D., of Project Resilience

In 30 first-person accounts, teens tell how they overcame major life obstacles. As teens read this book, they will discover they're not alone in facing life's difficulties. They'll also learn about seven resiliencies—insight, independence, relationships, initiative, creativity, humor, and morality—that everyone needs to overcome tough times. For ages 13 & up. *$14.95; 192 pp.; softcover; 6" x 9"*

The Teenagers' Guide to School Outside the Box

by Rebecca Greene

This practical, inspiring book explores the world of alternative learning, giving teens the knowledge and tools they need to make good choices. The author introduces and describes a world of possibilities, from study abroad to internships, apprenticeships, networking, job shadowing, service learning, and many more. For ages 13 & up. *$15.95; 272 pp.; softcover; illust.; 6" x 9"*

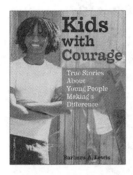

Kids with Courage
True Stories About Young People Making a Difference
by Barbara A. Lewis
Eighteen remarkable kids speak out, fight back, come to
the rescue, and defend their beliefs.
$12.95; 184 pp.; softcover; B&W photos, 6" x 9"

Wise Highs
How to Thrill, Chill, & Get Away from It All Without Alcohol
or Other Drugs
by Alex J. Packer, Ph.D.
The best-selling author of *How Rude!*® describes more
than 150 ways to feel really, really good—naturally,
safely, and creatively. From breathing and meditation to
exercise and sports, gardening, music, and games, these
are "highs" that can change teens' lives without leaving
them dull, burned out, or hung over. Includes updated
resources. Ages 13 & up.
$15.95; 264 pp.; softcover; illust.; 7¼" x 9¼"

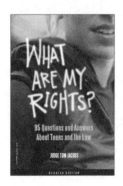

What Are My Rights? (Updated Edition)
95 Questions and Answers About Teens and the Law
by Thomas A. Jacobs, J.D.
"How long do I have to stay in school?" "Can my property
be searched and seized?" "Are my grades public information?" "When can I have a beer?" "What if I'm discriminated against?" Teens often have questions about the
law, but they don't know where to turn for answers.
Updated with new facts and resources, written in clear,
everyday language, this book explores 95 legal questions
that pertain specifically to teens. Includes questions for
reflection and discussion. Ages 12 & up.
$14.95; 208 pp.; softcover; 6" x 9"

To place an order or to request a free catalog of
SELF-HELP FOR KIDS® *and* SELF-HELP FOR TEENS® *materials,*
please write, call, email, or visit our Web site:

Free Spirit Publishing Inc.
217 Fifth Avenue North • Suite 200 • Minneapolis, MN 55401-1299
toll-free 800.735.7323 • local 612.338.2068 • fax 612.337.5050
help4kids@freespirit.com • www.freespirit.com

Fast, Friendly, and Easy to Use
www.freespirit.com

Browse the catalog

Info & extras

Many ways to search

Quick check-out

Stop in and see!

Our Web site makes it easy to find the positive, reliable resources you need to empower teens and kids of all ages.

The Catalog.
Start browsing with just one click.

Beyond the Home Page.
Information and extras such as links and downloads.

The Search Box.
Find anything superfast.

Your Voice.
See testimonials from customers like you.

Request the Catalog.
Browse our catalog on paper, too!

The Nitty-Gritty.
Toll-free numbers, online ordering information, and more.

The 411.
News, reviews, awards, and special events.

 Our Web site is a secure commerce site. All of the personal information you enter at our site—including your name, address, and credit card number—is secure. So you can order with confidence when you order online from Free Spirit!

For a fast and easy way to receive our practical tips, helpful information, and special offers, send your email address to upbeatnews@freespirit.com. View a sample letter and our privacy policy at www.freespirit.com.

1.800.735.7323 • fax 612.337.5050 • help4kids@freespirit.com